ESSENTIALS

Bridging the Leadership Gap

BOBBY BOGARD

DEDICATION

This book is dedicated to Jesus Christ; the One who gave me life, invited me into His mission, and called me to become a multi-generational leader. Essentials is also dedicated to my amazing wife Rose, my children, their spouses and my grandsons. All of these incredible people have pushed me and been my inspiration to write this book.

CONTENTS

ACKNOWLEDGMENTS

I would be remiss if I thought that the writing of this book was solely based upon my competencies. Like many accomplishments in life, the involvement of others is the key to success. Many of the principles in this book relate to team, comradery, partnerships, and relationships. So, it is imperative that I recognize those who have pushed me forward, mentored me, and believed in the mission of my life. The contributions of those who are mentioned here cannot be measured nor can I express the depth of my love and appreciation to each one. I hope you will take the time to read this segment because it truly reflects the heart and soul of this book called, "Essentials."

The foundation of my life is built upon my personal relationship with Jesus Christ. While the forward describes the inception of our relationship, I want to say here that without Him I can't imagine where I would have journeyed. Cultural trends, research, and statistics concerning my personal profile prior to Christ paints a bleak picture of what my life could have entailed. Just the stats concerning children raised in a single parent home without a father are chilling. But, Jesus Christ changed my life. He has walked me through an amazing life of redemption and given me an incredible platform of leadership and influence. May He receive all the glory and honor!

My wife, affectionately known as "The Beautiful Rose of Texas," has walked with me through thick and thin. She spoke life into me during my lowest times. Rose is the epitome of Proverbs 31:11,12 (NLT) , especially the part, "she will greatly enrich his life." I am a much better father, a far greater man, and an exceedingly stronger leader because of her. This book is as much hers as it is mine because we lived "Essentials" together on so many levels. They say, "behind every good man is a good woman" and I know that to be true in my life. I could not imagine life without her.

My children are incredible. In many ways, they have been the "lab rats" for the writing of this book. They have been the recipients of both my ineptness and my proficiencies as a leader. The simple position of leadership has an impact upon the leader's children and I believe even more so in a ministry setting. Pastor's kids have high expectations heaped upon them. My kids have survived all of that and have become some astounding leaders in their own rights. I am amazed at their insights, their capacities, and their accomplishments. Rose and I wanted to live in such a way that our children would exceed our lives in every way. We have lived to see that happen over and over. "Essentials" is written today because they gave me permission to influence their lives, and because they have consistently challenged me to write my story. I could not be prouder of the legacy being lived out in their lives and the legacy being sown into our grandsons.

Elbert Pool led me to a relationship with Jesus Christ. Elbert was the faithful pastor of Gospel Mission Church in Des Arc, Arkansas until he re-fired... now he ministers at the senior citizen center and continues to share Christ at every opportunity. Elbert taught me to pray. Many times I would stop by to see him only to find him in the sanctuary crying out to God on behalf of people. Elbert taught me authentic worship. He worshipped from a deep place of knowing God and loving God. Elbert taught me to love the Word of God not simply as a book but as a living book that could change your life every day. He preached it from a relationship not from an exegetical thesis. He is my hero in the faith above all other men I have known. I am so thankful my formative years in the faith were under the influence of this man.

Another gift to my life was Jim Hodges. Jim intersected my life during two significant seasons. The first was at Christ for the Nations where I was a student and Jim was one of my professors. Jim was a great teacher and acknowledged by the students as one of their favorites. He was my favorite for sure. But the classroom was not the way God used Jim to impact my life. It was on the basketball court. Jim showed me that there is a humanity to leadership. Leaders are people. People make mistakes. Jim was extremely frustrated with the calls the refs were making… I was one of the refs in our intramural league and the ref making those calls. Although he never said anything out of order and he held his frustration in check, I knew he was steamed. He modeled humility, submission, and vulnerability which made his teachings all the more impactful to me. I learned that day that leadership involves more than a title, it's about a lifestyle. Jim also impacted my life years later when he opened up an opportunity for me to become a staff member at a megachurch. The staff position was an amazing opportunity but again God used Jim in a different setting to shape my life. It was in his home. Jim and his wife Jean opened their home to young leaders. We would gather, eat, talk, play, and the Hodges would pour into us. They modeled relational mentorship. Those days set a foundation of relational ministry into my heart. Jim would always say, "All ministry comes out of a relationship." I believe it to this day.

Spiritual fathers are a gift but so are spiritual siblings. Rose had formed a significant brother/sister relationship with Duane VanderKlok while we were students at Christ for the Nations. Over the years Duane and Jeanie became close friends. They would stop over and see us during their trips in and out of Mexico. Later in ministry the VanderKloks returned to Michigan and began pastoring what became Resurrection Life Church. During the early 1990's Duane invited me to become a staff member and we served there for almost 13 years as the Executive Pastor. Duane taught me leadership. How to communicate vision, how to handle conflict, how to manage money, how to create momentum, how to empower others, and how to influence. The church grew during that time from 1,500 to just over 7,000 in weekly attendance and we added almost 230,000 square feet to the facilities. Duane modeled consistency. He did not get caught up in the latest Christian teaching fad or wave of experience. He stayed true to the vision God gave him and refused distractions. As a result, we saw an annual growth rate of approximately 20%. Duane taught me the power of steadfastness and confidence. I am still in pursuit of those two qualities today.

Lastly, I want to acknowledge Tom Lane. Tom is a father. He has not only raised an amazing family, he has impacted many on a spiritual level. Early on in my walk with God, God gave me a sense that He had a calling on my life to be a "father to the fatherless." Astounding to me because I never had my earthly father be a significant part of my life. For the most part, he was absent and distant. So how could I become a "father to the fatherless?" Tom Lane entered my life after I had almost thirty years of ministry experience. Tom was the Executive Senior Pastor of Gateway Church when I joined their staff. The immediate impression you have of Tom is that he is a father, a statesman, and a pillar. Tom was my direct oversight for a season and it was in those interactions that Tom awakened the reality of the spiritual father that I was to become. Up to this point, I was recognized by several as a spiritual father, but I knew I was going to a new level and Tom was the example Father had put in front of me. I observed the way Tom discussed issues, the way he led our staff meetings, the way he addressed conflict, the way he drew people close, and the way he interacted with his own children. I took note of his values. I read his book. I absorbed as much as I could. To this day, I value every moment with Tom Lane.

These acknowledgments are a testimony to the pages that follow. We are truly better together, and these contributions to my life and many more validate that truth. But there must be a relational transaction for that to happen. We have to let people into our world, we have to be willing to be in their world, we have to understand the "Essentials" that make the relational transactions a reality. I heard a saying years ago that bears repeating here: "When the devil wants to destroy a destiny he sends a relationship, and when God wants to build a destiny He sends a relationship." John Maxwell put it this way, "Those closest to you will either make you or break you." The truth is that to reach our greatest potential we have to have people in our lives. That gets messy. Especially when you are seeking to build legacy. Legacy requires one generation to stand on the foundations of a previous generation, while seeking to become the cornerstone of future generations. Legacy happens when the young receive from the old and the old are willing to offer themselves to young. We need others. Others need us. My prayer is that this book, "Essentials", will offer you the tools to bridge the gap and experience the fulfillment of relational mentoring and leadership transference.

PREFACE
Bridging the Leadership Gap

Is a Leader Born or Made?

Is a leader born or is a leader developed? It's an age-old question. My answer is "yes." Yes a leader is born because there are certain innate characteristics that leaders possess. It is through those intuitive traits that a leader discovers that he or she desires to lead. I recall one such discovery in my own life. I was six years old and we had to catch a school bus every morning. Each morning when the bus would come into sight, I would start lining everyone up to get on. Why? Because I was born to lead.

However, that is not enough. A leader has to be developed. Leaders must travel through different seasons and walk through different experiences to become a well-rounded leader. Various skills must be honed to advance into a broader sphere of influence. It is imperative that leaders expand their pain capacity to endure the difficulties that are inevitable in leadership. Therefore, a leader is made through the process of relationships, experiences, education, opportunities, repetitions and more. For example, I had two similar learning experiences occurring just a few years apart. The first was the disappointment and discouragement when a person was brought in from the outside of our organization and given a position that I had been promised. The second was when I had launched a major initiative and successful program only to have it handed over to a subordinate to navigate its future. What was my takeaway after processing those events? My leadership strength is in the strategic planning, pioneering, entrepreneurial, building, and catalyst stages not in the long-haul maintenance and growth process. My leadership was discovered through the experiences I just described.

What you have in your hands or on your digital platform are the "Essentials" that I have discovered in my 45 plus years of leadership. However, this is not a book. You will discover that I jump from 3rd person to 1st person in each segment. I'm talking to young and unskilled leaders one minute and then addressing talented and seasoned leaders in the next. You will notice that I speak from the negative trait of certain leaders then turn around and address their positive qualities in the same text. As well, I move from insight to application throughout this writing. I have been asked, "Is this a book, a workbook, a series of blogs, or a personal development tool?" Again, my answer is "yes." This project will have the feel of all those elements. My desire is that one of them will help you understand that you were born to lead. My goal is that you will read and apply sections of this writing over and over. You were born a leader but you must become a leader in every new season of life. Enjoy the journey.

INTRODUCTION

This book began to be written on August 15, 1972. I was entering my junior year of high school and our blended family had recently moved to a little town in Arkansas. Des Arc was located about sixty-five miles east of Little Rock, off I-40 heading toward Memphis, Tennessee. Needless to say, I wasn't excited about the move. Little did I know it was a move that would forever change my life.

My stepfather's twin brother pastored a little church called Gospel Mission. Besides being disappointed with the move to this little town, I was really set back by the idea of church. During my previous seventeen years I had rarely interacted with any church. My experience up to that point left me less than impressed by any religious activity. I wasn't prepared for what I was about to encounter.

Gospel Mission gathered a group of about twenty teens between ages 12-18. When I met them, I had to acknowledge that there was something very different about them. They had no interest in my heroes, Cheech & Chong. They intrigued me. I decided to go on a trip that they were taking to a nearby town. Honestly, my interest in going was to get to know the Bruce girls. The trip slowly unfolded the reality that I wasn't even on the same page with this group of students. They talked about

Jesus as if He was in the car with us. They were pumped about sharing their testimonies of how Jesus had changed their lives. I was scared. I knew I didn't have a testimony... let alone even know Jesus. Wasn't He supposed to be some guy who carried sheep? At least the only picture I had seen of Him portrayed that image. Long story short, after only two weeks of exposure to this radical group of teens, I desperately wanted what they had. I wanted to know Jesus personally! Thus, the inception of this book on that August evening in 1972 when I surrendered my life to Him and His purpose for me.

I'm sixty-five years old and have over 45 years of leadership experiences as of this writing. When I look back, I see how God created me to lead. Every season of my life and every opportunity I have been given centers around leading; leading vision, leading strategic planning, leading teams, leading departments, leading leaders. Many times God positioned me to lead a span of two or three generations simultaneously. I remember working at a Farmer's Co-op in the Little Rock area. I was fresh out of Bible school and newly married. I had no knowledge of what the co-op was all about. I was simply trying to make a living and provide for my new bride. Shortly after taking the job, I found myself leading men twice my age as the newly promoted dock supervisor. Many of the ticket pullers and forklift drivers could have been my older brothers or dad. Yet here I was, leading them with only a few weeks under my belt. Why? Because I was called to lead.

Most of my ministry experience has been about leading. I am humbled by the favor that God put on my life. I would never have imagined that a boy from a broken home, who Jesus found in a little Arkansas town, could ever have the opportunity to lead on an executive level. Yet that has been my journey. I rose to senior leadership positions in every organization I served. Through the process of promotions, I would have the privilege to serve multiple generations. That has been a driving force within me... generational ministry. Bridging leaders from several generations to work for His Kingdom. Putting teams together by empowering the established leaders while providing emerging leaders opportunity to contribute. Building a succession pathway is imperative for any organization to flourish and have lasting influence.

One such experience happened at a mega church in the Dallas / Ft Worth area. I was serving on the executive team and had the opportunity to lead some businessmen. We put together small gatherings of business owners to help each other succeed. Although overall it did not achieve all I had hoped, there was one moment that made it all worthwhile. An older businessman was about to lose everything because of the economic crisis of that time. The calamity he was facing was severe. He had mentored many of our younger leaders and had assisted them in building their businesses. Those emerging leaders rallied to his aid. They helped him with new technology and assisted him in creating new delivery systems. His business endured and rallied to become more profitable than ever. This alone proved to me the power of generational influence and teamwork.

My desire is that this book will make a difference. I hope that the simple insights will build a bridge between established and emerging leaders. I wrote this book from the heart of a father. There are times in this book where I will push young leaders to broaden perspective and move away from entitlement attitudes. I also try to challenge veteran leaders to overcome their apprehension and engage with the developing leaders in their world. I offer suggestions to both generations and encourage implementation of the principles presented. I deeply believe the essentials presented within these pages will lift the leadership lid of every generation. I hope you feel the same after reading it.

Helping leaders and churches solve problems and succeed,
Bobby Bogard
Bogard Group Ministries
bogardgroup.com

ONE

Doing & Coaching

◄─────────────────────────►

IT IS ESSENTIAL FOR GROWING LEADERS TO DO THE WORK!

Emerging Leaders Can Contribute Now! They are young, vibrant, and eager to conquer their world. Their understanding of technology and social marketing alone sets them apart from many of their seasoned coworkers. These young leaders want to be decision makers, actively participate in strategic forums, and build companies that impact humanity for the good. So the following concepts are presented to ground the emerging leaders' zeal, while at the same time pry the stranglehold of empowerment out of the established leadership.

Emerging Leaders: Find Something to Do, And Do It! A young leader can be overlooked when they refuse menial opportunities. Empowerment is often withheld because the inexperienced apprentice sees the task at hand as being beneath them. They would do themselves a favor if they would put on the apron of a servant rather than the robe of a ruler. When something is considered to be beneath the emergent leader, their attitude toward the assignment could disqualify them from being offered the next opportunity. They fail to realize that someone before them paved the way for the company's success. That those individuals wore multiple hats and took on anything and everything to move the organization forward. If the emerging leader takes the same approach to assigned responsibilities, they will position themselves for a favorable future. This is more about attitude than aptitude. Seasoned leaders are more apt to work through a lack of skills or knowledge. However, a poor attitude toward work, sacrifice, team, or culture will only be tolerated for so long. Does the upstart have enough perspective to understand that everything contributes to the success of the organization? That is the question in the back of the owner's mind. Can this novice handle the small things with the same zeal and passion that greater responsibilities afford? Many young leaders have derailed their future by simply taking on the wrong orientation toward humble and humdrum assignments. Many times the best talents are discovered in the process of doing. When the growing leader takes on assignments that may not appear to be advancing their goals, they put their skill sets on display. Now the established leadership can observe their problem-solving skills. They can witness the maturing leaders ability to build a coalition or navigate themselves through conflict. Leaders will lead and others will follow whether the leader is leading down, laterally, or up; it makes no difference. By doing the task, thriving leaders will make their leadership evident to all.

Emerging Leaders: Learn to Serve

Developing leaders would do well to comprehend the power of serving the needs of others. No one likes a self-promoting, egotistical, and self-serving individual. When young leaders demonstrate the old adage; "There is no 'I' in Team," they will win the comradery necessary to advance. These evolving leaders must learn the reality that where they dream of going requires the involvement of other people. Not from the standpoint of using people, but in the framework of "we are better together." When they serve the needs of others, they are setting into motion the law of sowing and reaping. Scripture teaches that when you are faithful in another man's endeavors God will reward you with your own. So what does that look like? Firstly, it doesn't involve self-promotion, name dropping, speaking out of turn, dis-honoring peers, throwing others under the bus, or any other aspects of exalting self while demeaning others. It looks more like giving honor to whom honor is due. It is championing the cause of others. Many times it involves the character demonstrated when no one else is observing. Serving others needs is about making sure everything is completed and on time. That could mean being involved in something outside of their job description but necessary for the team to win the day. Secondly, present culture, much the same as cultures of the past, press emerging leaders to do whatever it takes to be #1 and never settle for second. That breeds a competitive spirit that makes everything about the individual. Again, it becomes more about the attitude than the skill sets. It is cut-throat, backstabbing, sabotage, and destruction of others for the sole purpose of winning. It is not that winning or competing are wrong. Those are good qualities when they are contained and harnessed for the good of all not just the one. The team is not about the gathering of #1's to form a group of high-powered individuals. Rather, the team is about the meshing of extremely talented people for the purpose of combining talents to serve the mission. Now the focus is on the purpose of the individuals talent to make those around them better. Emerging leaders who fail to learn this lesson may advance but they will do so on a very lonely path.

Emerging Leaders: Listen Before You Speak

Another word of advice regarding attitude is found in the thought that "It is better to be seen than heard." While young leaders possess fresh ideas and perspectives, they must learn when to speak and when to speak without using words. Complaining about a lack of opportunity, voicing objections about the culture, or bemoaning the lack of personal preferences will only hinder. Displaying bad attitudes, pouting about being overlooked, or being combative toward their peers only makes them appear immature..... Wah wah wah.... Mama is not here! There seems to be a lack of honor and regard for statesmen, senior leaders, accomplished women, and elders. Social media has built a medium where anyone feels empowered to criticize, mock, attack, slam, and bad-mouth anyone or anything. Add to that the sense of entitlement and the mountain of disregard grows to seemingly insurmountable heights. Another contributor to this plight is the new commerce and business ventures created by online platforms. All of these factors collide in relational interactions that are required for complete transactions. Even if texting your resignation is the current trend, there is still the people factor that involves communication skills. When an individual learns to listen before they speak, they will speak from a holistic viewpoint. They may come to an understanding which could temper the emotions they originally felt in an interaction with a team member. And had they not been checked by what they heard, they could have demoralized a teammate by the tone of voice or language they used to address an issue. Listening can increase knowledge and empower the speaker with more authority whereas they may have been heard as a complete imbecil. The point is that healthy interaction in whatever medium requires the ability to hear and understand before spouting off an opinion. While this point is a push against the tide of present culture, it seems to be sound counsel for those wanting to grow into a leadership position.

> Many young leaders have derailed their future by simply taking on the wrong orientation toward humble and humdrum assignments.

It is essential for established leaders to coach.

Established Leaders: Be Willing to Coach, Not Critique! Remember, there was a time when you were advancing through the ranks. Stop and think about that one person who took you "under their wings." The one who believed in you and gave you opportunity. They credited you with enough moxy to give you a project to manage. When you failed, they encouraged you. When you succeeded they celebrated you. They shaped your leadership and made you better. Emerging leaders are crying out for coaches, mentors, and someone who will believe in them. The last thing they need is someone who only sees their weakness, critiques their every move, and only offers correction. The constant barrage of criticism demoralizes their dreams and embeds a sense of failure, the inability to measure up.

You too were a novice at one time. Don't expect perfection. Be willing to invest in the raw talent. Become comfortable with messy things. Developing leaders are just that, developing! They will make mistakes. They will be overconfident. They will push your limits. But they are worth it. These up and coming leaders are the future of the company and the mission. When you create an atmosphere where failure is permitted, you give them room to grow. Each hurdle they overcome fuels their ability to lead. Help them by discussing the difficulties. Challenge them to work through tedious issues and relational conflicts. Coach them to see things from different perspectives to gain better awareness. The goal is to help them grow.

> Developing leaders
> would do well to
> comprehend the power
> of serving the needs of
> others.

Established Leaders: Be Willing to Model Not Mock!

Demonstrate mature leadership. There is an old saying, "It's more caught than taught." These young leaders have book knowledge and passion. Now they need some intense OJT (on the job training). What they don't need is someone who mocks their lack of experience, someone who ridicules their inability to practically apply what they learned in the classroom, or someone who taunts them when they run up against a difficult problem. When you have an oversight meeting ask them questions that require critical thinking. Respond with stories and personal examples… remember, they have read the books.

Focus on the <u>why</u> more than the <u>how</u>. Why you chose to use a particular strategy to fund an initiative. Why you involved some departments and not others in the strategic planning processes. Help them comprehend why you chose a vendor who presented the highest bid over a more budget friendly one. Model vulnerability by sharing your mishaps, your weaknesses, and your successes. Call their attention to other leaders in the company that exemplify best practices. Show them how, watch them do it, do it with them and then allow them to do it with others. Always push them to be their best and represent your best in their presence. The mission is to build them not break them.

> When an individual
> learns to listen before
> they speak, they will
> speak from a holistic
> viewpoint.

Established Leaders: Be Willing to Interact Not React!

Spend the time. True coaching requires timely interactions. Some can be scheduled with oversight meetings but many others should take place in the context of real-life situations. Look for those teachable moments that require you to get out of the regular routine and give immediate attention to strategic details. An interaction of 30 minutes to an hour may cost some precious time for that day, but the growth in the emerging leader may save you countless hours of productivity in the future. However, be on guard for reactive responses that show anger or disgust. Teachable moments can deteriorate into setbacks quickly if failure is communicated. A reactive setback could cost the company the unrealized potential of that young leader because they quit. Whatever the case may be, you can only coach, mentor, or consult by using time as your friend not your enemy. It may involve taking time to discuss a better way of approaching an objective. Sometimes you may want to pull them aside during an assignment and coach them on how to maximize relational equity within the team. Taking the time to interact communicates value, it reassures them they are supported, it allows them to probe for better solutions, and it establishes the culture of honor needed to transfer knowledge. The purpose is to give them access.

> Don't expect perfection. Be willing to invest in the raw talent. Become comfortable with messy things.

<u>Established Leaders: Be Willing to Believe Not Bemoan!</u>
Believe in them. They are the future. Emerging leaders need affirmation. When you give them specific insights concerning their contribution to a successful venture, you push them forward. Resist the temptation to bemoan their naivety. Refuse to deplore their immaturity. Reject the notions that they are not worth the effort. Never underestimate your influence on these prospective leaders. Earlier you remembered your coach, your leader, your mentor who took you as you were and invested into you. Now, today, you have the opportunity to take on the raw talent before you and build a great leader. It's

your turn and your time to create a legacy of leaders who will take on the future. They will reach into new realms of possibilities because you built a platform to launch them ahead. Believe. Believe in what you are yet unable to see. Believe. Believe in your opportunity to make a difference. Believe. Believe in them and believe in yourself. The objective is to build visionaries. Recognize that your words are powerful! Choose them wisely when offering corrections. You can be straight forward but be sure you are attacking the issue and not the individual. When you touch someone's inner person with sharp, condescending, and demeaning words, you can scar them for life. There are so many wounded leaders whose mentors were rash with their criticism, who used unnecessary analogies, and who failed to recognize the power of their influence. Speak the truth in love. Respect the individual. Allow yourself to err on the side of graciousness. Build up, don't tear down. Lift them to the next level through conversations that focus on their success. Speak life. Speak faith. Speak to their potential not their present incompetence. The end game is to see them reach the maximum capacity of their God given talent.

Taking the time to interact communicates value!

Making it Real:

There was a season where I was bi-vocational. I was in an entrepreneurial endeavor and the beginning stages of building an organization. There wasn't enough cash flow to sustain my family so I had to take on a second vocation simultaneously. When I was a youth my stepdad had a construction business and I learned that trade. So here I was working eight to ten-hour days building homes and then giving attention to my start up in my spare time. This was a difficult season to say the least. Trying to navigate my family, my job, and my dream. But leaders do what they have to do to get from point A to point B.

One day I came into work and the builder informed me that his work had run out and that we would be shut down for a while. My budget and needs could not afford "a while." I had to find some income. That is when the most humbling job fell into my lap. I began to sell "twirl-n-ads!" Exactly, what is a "twirl-n-ad?" Well it is a plastic fan that slipped over a four-inch post with a magnetic base and it had inserts to advertise cars for sale. "WE FINANCE" "TODAY'S DEAL" "DISCOUNTED" and the list went on. They were bright yellow, grass green, and fluorescent red. I had to walk onto a car lot like they were the greatest invention since the iPhone (well it wasn't around then). Funny thing was I had some friends who observed my tenacity, my commitment, my management of responsibilities, and my passion to do whatever it took to launch my dream. They invested financially and I was glad their support made my "twirl-n-ad" experience relatively short lived. I think my wife was thankful as well.

ESSENTIALS

So what is to be learned from my story?

1. Work is not a bad four-letter word. It is a necessity for achievement.
2. Talents that you acquire along the way can be the keys to unlocking dreams.
3. You need others to move to the next level or the next season. In my story that was the builder, the person who invented "twirl-n-ads," and my friends who invested in our story.
4. Leaders do what others are unwilling to do.

Emerging Leaders Action Items:

1. Reflect on your attitude about the current role that you play. Make a list of the responsibilities that you often put off until the last minute (procrastination).
2. If you were your oversight, what behaviors would you address with yourself?
3. Now take out your phone and record a conversation that your think your oversight would have with you to help you improve.

Established Leaders Action Items:

1. Who invested in your leadership development? Choose two significant influences.
2. Describe the immaturity or lack of experience and knowledge that they addressed that changed your leadership paradigm.

3. Schedule an appointment with someone in your leadership team that struggles in that area and do for them what your mentors did for you.

Remember:

- Many times the best talents are discovered in the process of doing. By doing the task, thriving leaders will make their leadership evident to all.
- Servant leadership is about championing the cause of others.
- Focus on the Why more than the How.
- True coaching demands timely interactions.
- Respect the individual. Allow yourself to err on the side of graciousness.

TWO

Lanes & Plateaus

←——————————————————→

IT IS ESSENTIAL FOR EMERGING LEADERS TO KNOW & PROTECT THEIR STRENGTH!

Every Emerging Leader must know their lane, their sweet spot, their niche! Leaders are not an accident waiting to happen. Leaders refuse to take up space and consume oxygen. They are purposeful and deliberate in their approach to their mission. Why? Because they understand their center, the focus of their strengths. Developing leaders should be on a constant pursuit to discover and enhance their strong points.

Finding the sweet spot begins with an acknowledgement of God as Creator.

➔ Psalm 139:16 in the Message Bible reads, "Like an open book, You watched me grow from conception to birth; all the stages of my life were spread out before You, the days of my life all prepared before I'd even lived one day."

➔ The Apostle Paul recognized this truth when he wrote to the Galatians and made this statement, "But even

17

before I was born, God chose me and called me by His marvelous grace." Galatians 1:15 (NLT).

There is a God thing in each person that makes life worth living. Every person has been hardwired with a specific set of attributes that contribute to their specific purpose in life. Some leaders make it look easy to strategize and formulate specific initiatives. Others can orchestrate systems and processes that enhance productivity and maximize talent. It's all in their DNA if you will, that center or blueprint which the Creator put within them.

Several things are set into place when a young developing leader acknowledges their Creator:

1. They seek God as the source of their strength.
2. They carry themselves with humility because of their dependence upon God.
3. They come to understand that one day of His favor is worth more than 1,000 days of their labor.
4. They utilize their talents for His purpose.

A leader's sweet spot is the lane of life where maximum results take place. It is the leader's life purpose. The sweet spot is where their natural talents, core values, and life experiences align to define their assigned mission. It is a convergence of personal passions, divine favor, and acquired wisdom which shapes the leader's purpose.

There are several indicators that bring a leader's sweet spot into view. While these markers are not rocket science, they do go unnoticed or undervalued quite often. Once seen and applied they can provide the guidance needed to maximize the leader's niche. Developing leaders should visit these principles on a regular basis because they will help make needed adjustments along the way. Here are some suggestions to make the discovery process easier:

> Finding the sweet spot begins with an acknowledgement of God as Creator.

→ Recognize Passion

There is a great question that will generate this thought process: "What gets you up in the morning?" If it's just the alarm clock to another day of drudgery at the office, then passion is likely missing. What is the dream? What is the vision? What is cherished at the core will be aimed at with a life! So, if failure wasn't possible, if money wasn't an obstacle, if it was a sure thing, what would the desire look like? Now write that down in seven words or less! Why? Because 70% of the workforce hate their job and are unmotivated.

- Eric Little: 1924 Summer Olympics, *"When I Run, I feel His Passion"*
- Martin Luther King, Jr., *"I Have A Dream!"*
- Avengers Movie, *"I am Groot!"*

Here is where an established leader can be utilized. These men and women have lived life at so many different levels. As a result, they can ask the right questions. One question asked at the right time can change everything. Seasoned leaders can perceive and discern hidden talents. They have the power to call that out in an emerging leader. An eager novice leader should ask themselves, "Who are the patriarchs around me that can help me see what I don't see?" Experienced leaders know what it's like to carry a burning passion. They understand the frustration of not having an avenue to express it or release it. They can describe what it was like to rein in their zeal and learn the virtue of patience. Their tenure as a leader has taught them that they are only one relationship away from living out their passion.

→ Define Non-negotiables
   There are some things that are built-in red lights. These are the non-negotiables. They define the boundaries of integrity. Non-negotiables are the core values that, if violated, the result is moral compromise. These become the guidelines to decision making. They allow the leader to possess answers before questions are even asked. When difficult choices have to be made a set of ethics exist to guide the leader to the best solution. A code of behavior keeps the leader in check emotionally and relationally. The leader's principles and standards direct their judgement of what is important in life. Young leaders would do well for themselves to define their personal non-negotiables. They will alleviate unethical conduct, moral compromise, and foolish choices.

Defining the core beliefs is a must.

- So, make a list of non-negotiables
  - How will you engage with the opposite sex and what boundaries will you set for those interactions?
  - How will you handle money when it comes to things like per-diems, personal expenses, mileage reimbursements, and even taxes.
  - How will you conduct business with others regarding percentages, profit margins, product quality, contract negotiations, and general business practices?
  - How will you relate to people socially, in the workplace, or at home?

- Write a motto for each core value to solidify its meaning.
  - For example: **Generosity** - Steward resources knowing they are His.
  - For example: **Serve** - Help others fulfill their mission.

Senior leaders can help with this exercise. They have seen the rise and fall of leaders in their field. They can describe in detail what a moral fall entails and the devastation that follows. These women and men have faced the danger of compromise in their own life. Their stories and experiences can become guardrails for growing leaders.

Veteran leaders can give definition to values that have kept them strong. They can help emerging leaders build the non-negotiables that will serve them well in difficult seasons. They understand that firm convictions not only keep you from trouble but they also strengthen one's resolve to succeed.

→ Identify Talents

What comes natural? What abilities are noticed by others that seem normal? The talents and skills of a leader are easily recognized by others. Yet, because they are so familiar to the leader, they may be taken for granted. The importance of identifying talent really comes down to maximizing a leader's normal skills. Understanding personal competencies protects the leader from comparing themselves with other talents in the room. Confidence is found when one discovers their areas of expertise. It allows them to focus themselves on strength development rather than wasting time on their weaknesses. Someone once noted that a leader should live in their strengths and hire or recruit to their weaknesses. When a leader tries to run in a lane outside of their natural skills it's inevitable that they will burn out. The question each growing leader should ask themselves is, "What do I do well?"

- Ask friends and family to compile a list of your talents and skills.
- Now, take the list and pray for Father to show you your top three.
- Make a growth plan for each to be executed over the next six months.
- Recruit a mentor or coach to assist in the process.

Here again, established leaders can add value. Because leaders assess talent all the time they see things from a different vantage point. Not only can they see obvious skills they can see raw talent as well. Young leaders who seek out mentors will find exponential growth occurs. Professional athletes are admired for their talent. Yet, even Tiger Woods employs a coach. Someone who can observe, identify, and instruct the athlete toward improvement. Established leaders have resources, connections, and experience that will elevate an emerging leader's growth trajectory. Once talent is identified it has to be developed. Some would say there are two schools of development: 1) school of hard knocks or on the job training 2) school of learning from others. Both serve the student well. Baseball is a great example. A developing batter must have reps (times at bat facing a pitcher) but they also need a hitting coach. The reps give them experience and the hitting coach tweaks their skills or technique. Emerging leaders who recruit a coach and use their talents will naturally become better.

→ Remember Experiences
   There is something about the power of memory that reinforces our sweet spot. David put this into action when he went out to face Goliath. "I have killed a lion and a bear!" He fortified his personal aptitude to sling a stone by remembering. Recalling our victories is vital to sustaining momentum or generating courage to move forward. At some point, every leader faces the unavoidable question, "Do I have what it takes to succeed?" An advancing leader should take note of the wins in their life. Who was there? What skill was enhanced? Why did success occur? How could that experience help in the future? Everything, positive and

negative, that they have been through culminates to build character, sharpen skills, teach lessons, expand influence, and create pathways of growth. There is nothing lost in life when it is remembered in the right context. Memorials are created to remember an event. When the event is remembered then the who, the what, the why, and the how are clarified.

- What are the memorials that need to be recorded? Take some time to reflect.
- As events come to mind, write down what you remember.
- Ask questions to identify how that event developed your sweet spot.
- When a "defeat" took place, ask the Holy Spirit how He is taking that and turning it into a victory for your future.
- Remember.

Established leaders would say, "Journal more." Write it down. History is a great guide for gaining true perspective. Memory is a gift to recall. Past victories are an encouragement that present obstacles can be overcome. Even painful memories can serve as motivation to keep moving forward. Emerging leaders who record their journey will discover how people, experiences, training, unforeseen circumstances, and choices shaped them to live out their mission in life. Write. Record. Journal. Write some more.

History is a great guide
for gaining true
perspective. Memory is a
gift to recall. Past
victories are an
encouragement that
present obstacles can be
overcome.

There are two major threats a leader must contend with to stay in their sweet spot!

The first is comparison. *This topic cannot be over communicated.* An emerging leader demeans their calling by scaling it against others. Comparison only leads to one of two conclusions: insecurity or pride. Either focus will lead the developing leader into a mishap. Their mission and purpose can either be lost or destroyed by this disease. When comparison leads to insecurity the leader will tend to defer authority. They will struggle to make decisions. Insecure leaders lack the courage to make the tough calls. Prideful leaders assume the opposite. They see themselves as above common mistakes. They demean the talent around them. A proud leader will tend to be a top down leader. Comparison is a killer of truth. Comparison is incapable of an accurate analysis of skills, experience, talent, and relational equity. The apostle Paul discouraged comparison, pointing out that those who engaged in it were not wise. Emerging leaders must secure their identity and become comfortable in their own skin.

Secondly is compromise. *Compromise will lead to a forfeit of principles and convictions*. Once compromise is put into play a young leader will either A) lead a life filled with lies or B) lose all their influence on others. Compromise usually begins with a lie that says, "only this once," or "no one will know." The bible says that "the heart is deceitful above all else and desperately wicked." (Jeremiah 17:9) It is so easy for the heart of a leader to be swayed unless they have established their convictions, values, and personal lines of integrity. The carnage around a fallen leader is demoralizing. A developing leader should predetermine their ethics and morals prior to any assignment or mission.

These two threats never go away. Young leaders must understand that their battles with comparison and compromise are lifelong. Every new season provides new personalities, new co-workers, and new relationships. Comparison and compromise lurk in each of those seasons. Their mission is to derail leaders. Prospective leaders who find their sweet spot will run in their lane, stay in their zone, and have their greatest impact. They will learn to find contentment in each phase of their journey. Growing leaders will refuse to be restricted by these two enemies.

Making it Real:

I was shocked when I hung up the phone. Did that conversation really just happen? What am I going to do with this? I was embarrassed. I was afraid. I was confused. The call was from an unknown woman. She related how she noticed that I had been looking at her throughout my presentation. She wanted me to know that she was interested in getting to know me better. I'm married! I have two kids! I don't know what she is talking about! I'm thankful that I had some non-negotiables solidified in my life at that moment. Others may have allowed their curiosity and fantasies rule the day. Not me. I went straight to my oversight's office and informed them of the call. I made myself accountable. I instructed my Administrative Assistant on how to screen calls and minimize that ever happening again. My non-negotiable saved my job, my marriage, and my integrity.

So what is to be learned from my story?

1. Pre-determined boundaries protect you.
2. True accountability provides a sense of security.
3. Have a person in your life where you can unpack emotions and be vulnerable.

Emerging Leaders Action Items:

1. "Chazown," by Craig Groeschel. Read It.
2. Complete the exercises within this chapter.
3. Talk to a mentor or coach about your insights.

Established Leaders Action Items:

1. Complete the exercises in this chapter.
2. Pull a team of leaders together and talk about comparison and compromise.

Remember:

- ☿ A leader's sweet spot is the lane of life where maximum results take place.
- ☿ What is cherished at the core will be aimed at with a life!
- ☿ One question asked at the right time can change everything.
- ☿ Emerging leaders who recruit a coach and use their talents will naturally become better.
- ☿ Write. Record. Journal. Write some more.
- ☿ Insecure leaders lack the courage to make the tough calls. Prideful leaders assume the opposite. They see themselves as above common mistakes. They demean the talent around them.

THREE

Relationships & Attitudes

Emerging leaders are the hope for any organization!
These young developing leaders will become the legacy of the
present established leadership. Hopefully, they find themselves
in an organization that develops, empowers, and releases up-
and-coming leadership. Otherwise, the company will plateau
and eventually die as the present leadership ages out. The death
of any organization is the failure to raise up the succeeding
generation of influencers. Newly empowered leadership can
produce fresh ideas, initiate resourceful systems, spawn
creative innovations and generate new income streams.
However, if the old regime is bent on retaining the status quo
and keeping the young leaders under their control, the
company will begin to decline as the changes in culture and
society move forward and leave them behind.

The opposite is true for an organization that embraces the
future and sets the stage for the next generation. These
institutions understand that change is inevitable. They grasp
the reality that sticking to the motto, "this is the way we've
always done it" is a slow path to self-inflicted irrelevance and
corporate suicide. These companies, churches, and businesses

seek out the best young leaders and invest in them. They are passionate about bridging the gap between what is and what will become. There is no fear in giving the young and inexperienced a place to flourish. Truth be known, they relish in the success of their younger peers. Should the budding leader be fortunate enough to land in such a place, they should look to cultivate the following essentials, as they seek to advance and expand their influence.

Established leaders would do well for themselves by modeling and imparting these crucial attributes to their successors.

It's essential to invite others into the journey!

A developing leader has a choice: *SOLO or SQUAD*

Many leaders take the solo route. Being the boss, making all the decisions, commanding the troops, and leading from the top down. Solo leadership is easier because decisions can be made quickly without any outside interference. However, leading alone wastes an abundance of wisdom and creative resources residing in others. The solo leadership style will automatically create silos within the organization; each silo vying for its own rewards, recognitions, and respect from their premier leader. Solo leaders are restricted by their own limitations. They bring only one source of influence, creativity, or insight to the table. Solo leaders tend to be insecure and threatened by others. They are guarded. They are suspicious. They are isolated. Young leaders who follow this path put a lid on their potential. There is a phrase that reveals this reality: "We are better together." Solo leaders are not together, they are alone. Solo leaders never experience the pain of growth created by diversity of thought and experience because they are always the smartest person in the room. They can't be challenged by the perspective of others because they only see things one way, theirs. Solo leaders hurt others. They crush the dreams of those around them because of their anxiety regarding success. Solo leadership is selfish leadership. Solo leadership stifles emerging leaders who tend to move on to either do their own thing or join another entity that values their contribution. Solo leadership is easier but far more costly in the long run.

> Established leaders
> would do well for
> themselves by modeling
> and imparting these
> crucial attributes to
> their successors.

Choosing to lead with a squad or a team is much messier. Decisions face scrutiny and sometimes take longer. There is push back, confrontation, conflict, and complexity. People are involved. They speak, they disagree, they dream, they have passion, and they are diverse. People bring emotion, ambition, suggestions, aggravations, and scrutiny. The Squad leader must cast vision and build team buy-in. Vision requires the leader to seek God, search out counsel, look into the future, and define the mission. People will buy into the leader before the vision, but the vision will keep the team together for the long haul. Squad leadership writes the vision and makes it plain so those who read it can run with it. A team requires the leader to position teammates in the right role. Coworkers can desire the same position, they can compete for the same opportunity, or they can have unrealistic expectations. Attitudes must be kept in check. Unity must be maintained. Ambitions must be managed. Squad leaders have to empower others for success. *Trust must be built at all levels*. Squad leadership requires tough calls. It's filled with pain and it demands confidence. Squad leaders must possess great communication skills, people skills, and management skills. Communication must be well thought out and clearly conveyed. People have to feel valued and appreciated. Systems and processes must be managed so that they do not encumber the Squad but rather empower it. Because in the end, the Squad will far out produce and build greater influence than any Solo leadership model.

The greatest potential of any leader will only be realized by understanding that they need others to attain it. *The graveyards are full of unrealized potential*. Leaders who were determined to make it on their own. People who were too insecure to ask for help. Companies limited by owners threatened with the success of others. Churches capped by pastors/leaders unwilling to empower those around them. Leaders who put a lid on their influence because they bought into the deception of leading SOLO.

Two Things that drive emerging leaders to go SOLO.

1. <u>Insecurity</u> --- *They choose to be a SOLO leader because they feel threatened by successful peers.* They gather followers who will never challenge their authority or champion other strategies to success. Solo leaders use authority to stifle the potential in their ranks. They feel if their weaknesses are exposed they will lose credibility. These insecure leaders refuse to empower others for fear they will succeed and take the spotlight. There is a high turnover rate under their leadership.

The SQUAD never develops under insecure leaders.

2. <u>Comparison</u> --- *They default to SOLO leadership because they are blinded by their need for approval or the entrapment of personal pride.* Their teams never have a sense of value because they want and take all the credit. They continually check the pecking order to see who might be a challenge to their position. Jealousy and envy corrupt the culture and displace unity. Their teams fail to fully contribute because they are always trying to "one-up" everyone around them. The comparison virus is forever driving them to make it on their own. They have a driving passion to be on top and therefore control all perceived threats. They cannot see the value of a team because they are blinded by "I."

The SQUAD gets overshadowed by the self-centered leader.

RELATIONSHIPS & ATTITUDES

Two things that inspire emerging leaders to recruit a SQUAD.

1. <u>Teamwork Makes the Dreamwork</u> --- *They become a SQUAD leader because they learn to respect talent. They regard the successes of others as a win for all.* Squad leaders are confident and work hard to build a team around their weaknesses. They understand that a well-rounded team can accomplish far more than any individual. They appreciate diversity and the resulting success it brings. Squad leaders empower their teams to succeed, and then acknowledge them when they win. They build processes and pathways for individuals to grow and advance. They learn to position team members in their sweet spot and then resource them to accomplish their mission.

They never go SOLO because they understand the effectiveness of a team.

2. <u>Companionship Makes the Work Fun</u> --- *They choose to be a SQUAD leader because working with a team is fun!* They create an environment of honor and esteem. Squad leaders minimize politics. They create a culture of family. They prioritize relationships over processes. Squad leaders know the power of passion. They reward contributions and honor achievements. They build opportunities for advancement. They exalt the "power of we" and minimize the "power of me." They celebrate the team. They have fun together.

They never go SOLO because they never replace Team with "I."

What can present leaders do to assist the emerging leaders as they navigate the choices between Solo or Squad leadership?

<u>**Established leaders have a choice**</u>: <u>STIFLE</u> or <u>STIMULATE</u>

It's easy for an established leader to stifle rising leaders. They worked hard to create the culture of their company. Their title alone influences everything around them. A seasoned leader can become comfortable. The voices of new leaders can irritate them, making them uncomfortable. It is easier to suppress new ideas rather than engage and empower emerging leaders to implement them. Tenured leaders love the status quo. They are secure with the way things are and hate change. Stifling leaders smother creativity. They resist innovation. They are looking for retirement rather than recalibration. They are an emerging leader's worst nightmare.

Stimulating new leaders to reach for their dreams means work. Stimulating others means to encourage, to challenge, to inspire them to greatness. A seasoned leader would be required to be present, to invest time, and in some seasons become vulnerable. Encouraging advancing leaders also means embracing new ideas, considering new systems, and allowing for change. All of these are uncomfortable to embedded leaders.

Succession is a requirement for any organization, family, or church to live beyond its present leadership.

If established leaders want to do anything more than make a name for themselves, they must stimulate young leaders not stifle them. Seasoned leaders who commit to the idea of succession will in turn commit to stimulating the next generation to take their lead. They will energize the transition by opening up to change while at the same time managing non-negotiables. They will empower young leaders but also offer coaching and mentorship. They commit to evolutionary processes and timelines. They are willing to hand over appropriate authority. These leaders stimulate change by modeling the past while embracing the future.

> Leading Solo wastes an abundance of wisdom and creative resources residing in others.

While extraordinary leaders stimulate progress and set up the next generation of leaders to emerge, apprehensive leaders will stifle any semblance of succession and seek to retain business as usual. Why the stark contrast? Why do some stifle and suppress?

ESSENTIALS

Two Things that drive experienced leaders to STIFLE:

1. <u>Fear</u> ----- *They STIFLE others because they are
   afraid of the future.* They question what would
   happen if a younger leader succeeded below them.
   Would they lose their authority? Tenured leaders do
   not believe their capacity to lead is over and feel they
   have more to contribute. However, they can fear
   becoming obsolete. They may sense the world passing
   them by and can become overwhelmed with the speed
   of change. They wonder if they will be discarded if they
   fail to control the emerging challenges? Their past
   becomes a refuge of security and the future looms as a
   threat to their self-worth. There is a struggle for
   personal identity. These leaders may even experience
   panic attacks for the first time in their lives. Young and
   successful leaders become their enemy instead of their
   legacy. They suppress anything and anyone perceived
   as a threat to their status, their security or their
   standing. They are afraid. They feel out of control.
   They question. Fear has them captive and they strike
   out against everything and everyone related to
   transformation and change.

**They are apprehensive and afraid to STIMULATE up
and coming leaders.**

2. <u>Selfishness</u> ---- *They STIFLE others because it
   means giving themselves.* They are comfortable.
   They paid their dues. Many established leaders are set
   in their ways. Change is the last thing they seek.
   Emerging leaders are an inconvenience. Building a

path for succession requires work, strategic planning, time, leadership development, loss of control, releasing authority, financial investment, and the stress of possible failure or, even worse, the opportunity for success. They see the risk totally on their side of the ledger. They have everything to lose and seemingly nothing to gain. Why go there? They enjoy their pace of life, their title, and their influence. Once they gave everything to the company and now the company owes them. They feel entitled to take it easy, after all, they did the hard work to get things to where they are now.

They are unwilling to STIMULATE growing leaders because of personal cost.

Two Things that inspire established leaders to Stimulate:

1. Legacy ---- *They STIMULATE others to build a legacy.* They understand the power of generational transference. They desire to move the mission forward for future impact. They are accomplished leaders with a passion to build a succession plan and recruit new leaders into the process. They stimulate the dreams, the passions, and the motivations of growing leaders. These are the seasoned leaders who give opportunity to others. They invest themselves to mentor next generation leaders. These amazing men and women understand they stood on the shoulders of past leaders in order to succeed. Now, they are relentless to provide the foundation for succeeding leaders to inherit the tools necessary for success in

their own missions. They celebrate when the up-and-coming exceeds expectations. They honor those who fight through disappointments and continue to lead. They build up those who experience failure and help them regain momentum. They cheer on those who take on what seemingly is impossible. These are legacy leaders. They know time and experience has shaped them but what they leave behind in the lives of their families, their apprentices, and their organizations will be what defines them.

They refuse to STIFLE emerging leaders because the future depends on them!

2. <u>Impact</u> ---- *They STIMULATE others for maximum impact.* Seasoned leaders want to leave their mark. They arrived where they are by including others. They realize that if they are to "go out with a bang," they must stimulate the best in their young leadership. Their greatest impact will be realized by unleashing current thoughts, sanctioning fresh strategy, and permitting apprentice leaders to participate. Concurrently, they know and understand that youth with seasoned oversight will have a higher rate of influence than novices left to themselves. There are things they know that inexperienced leaders do not. Intellectual knowledge must be balanced by experiential knowledge. They commit themselves to a mentorship process that allows both streams of thought to benefit the other. Succession of leadership is best built in the house of learning, supported by mutual honor and respect. Proven leaders shaping

growing leaders. Emerging leaders enlightening their predecessors. These legacy building women and men create a culture of trustworthiness and esteem. They value people. They respect talent. They recognize diversity. They compel trust. They pursue legacy from a position of character over charisma. They stimulate developing leaders to build on firm foundations, to forge new pathways, and to extend the life and influence of the organization.

They refuse to STIFLE young leaders because they understand the contributions young leaders can make.

IT'S ESSENTIAL TO UNDERSTAND THAT ATTITUDES IMPACT EVERY RELATIONSHIP!

Developing leaders need the right <u>ATTITUDE</u> to accomplish their ultimate purpose!

A prominent business school did a study of their graduates and found that 85% of their graduates' success was attributed to their attitude, while only 15% was attributed to their aptitude. How the leader reacts in any given situation will be influenced by their attitude. Their attitude will determine their success or failure. A leader with a self-centered attitude will demoralize the workforce. Leaders that are concerned about the welfare of the team will inspire productivity and draw out the best in others. When it comes to customer satisfaction, attitude makes all the difference. John Maxwell tells of seeing a sign in a service station entitled:

◆ **Why Customers Quit**...It read as follows:

> 1% Die, 3% Move Away, 5% Have Other
> Friendships, 9% Competitive Reasons (price), 14%
> Product Dissatisfaction, ***BUT***.... (here it comes)
> *68% Because of the Attitude of Indifference
> Toward Them by an Employee.*

Another example of the impact of one's attitude toward
leadership was discovered on the bumper of a car with a sign
that read. **"My Idea of Team is a Whole Lot of People
Doing What I Tell Them to Do"**

That's one attitude of leadership that many young leaders fall
into. However, it is the opposite of what Jesus modeled and
espoused when He said to His disciples, "You know that the
rulers of this world **lord it over their people**, and officials
flaunt their authority over those under them, but among you
it will be different. ***Whoever wants to be a leader among
you must be your servant***, and whoever wants to be first
among you must be the slave of everyone else. For even ***the
Son of Man came not to be served but to serve others*** and
to give His life a ransom for many."

**Jesus understood that people are not motivated by the
skills or the position a leader possesses, as much as they
are by the attitudes the leader demonstrates**.

There are many struggles that can move the attitude and
perspective of a leader in any given situation. Novice leaders
who learn to manage these pressure points will set themselves
up for success. These provocations can sway the emotions

from positive to negative or vice versa, depending on the attitude they ignite in the leader's life. No leader is immune to the pain of leadership. The question becomes are they able to handle the pain with the right attitude. It is imperative that developing leaders understand the source and impact of their attitudes.

THREE ATTITUDE STRESS POINTS FROM WITHIN:

1. **<u>Past Failure Leading to Fear of Failure</u>**. An emerging leader must develop the ability to turn defeat into a point of learning. Setbacks are painful and seek to define the growing leader as a failure. When the expected outcome is not met, a young leader cannot afford to allow the setback to be an indictment on their capabilities. New days bring new opportunities for success. Developing leaders should learn to deal with disappointment. They need to understand that success is always on the other side of difficulty and misfortunes. It is imperative they refuse to allow a defeatist attitude to take root in their soul. Fear has torment. A fearful attitude is a plague that ultimately destroys the capacity to lead.

Established leaders can help an emerging leader tackle fear. First, take time to know their story. If a young leader has experienced a recent failure, help them gain a well-rounded perspective. What a person believes to be true (true or not) can trap them into forecasting continued failure. Seasoned leaders should share their story of overcoming something similar. Let the growing leader know that there is life on the other side of adversities. The reinforcement of hope goes a long way to alleviating the fear of failure.

2. **Personal Identity Leading to Compromise**. How a young leader holds their personal identity is very important. Critics will always be available to judge the moment, but they never write the final chapter. The final chapter belongs to the emerging leader and it is yet to be written. Oversights may give an undesirable review, but they never have the power to script untapped potential. Leaders can cap opportunities by their lack of personal confidence. A growing leader will be challenged by the pecking order of their organization. They must resist the temptation to compare themselves. An emerging leader must fight to sustain their confidence and personal identity. The key to success and fulfillment does not rest in the hands of others. Success resides within the developing leader who pursues their dreams with confidence and conviction. Many young leaders allow their struggle with personal identity to push them to a prideful attitude.

Mature and knowledgeable leaders should make it a point to affirm their younger counterparts. So many developing leaders are void of a father's affirmation. They struggle with their personal identity because they have what one might call "an orphaned heart." They fight for affirmation. They struggle with confidence. They hunger for a parental figure, a mentor, or a coach that will encourage them, affirm them, and validate them. One moment, one word in season, one pat on the back can eradicate years of insecurity.

3. **Unrealized Expectation Leading to Discouragement.** Leaders constantly battle unfulfilled dreams. Why? Because leaders are dreamers. They are visionaries. They are driven to succeed. Young leaders are no exception. However, every dream won't come to pass. Prospective leaders will need to wrestle this demon to the ground because so much emphasis is put upon success. The need to conquer a challenge. The quest to make a name for themselves. The desire to climb the ladder of success. All of these are in the DNA of emerging leaders. However, the crash and burn can be fatal if they never learn to overcome. Pride haunts them. They are puffed up with success and devastated by failure. An emerging leader has to manage expectations.

Proven leaders have been through the ups and downs on numerous occasions. They have the enlightenment an emerging leader needs. Their experiences alone can be a source of encouragement and support. Although growing leaders will need to navigate their own battles, they can sidestep many pitfalls if an established leader will invest in them. A key to successful mentoring in this area is vulnerability. Will the seasoned leader be willing to share their failures? Are they willing to expose the weaknesses that existed in their leadership? Can they overcome their own pride and desire to impress or dominate? Veteran leaders can underestimate the power of their story and the impact of their words. The opportunity to develop an emerging leader can be a path to their own leadership legacy.

THREE ATTITUDE STRESS POINTS FROM WITHOUT:

1. <u>**Comparison**</u>. When leaders gather there is a common practice known as "measuring the room." It is a determination of the pecking order based upon whatever success factors are in play. The quest for validation motivates the up and coming leader to measure their current status against the standing of others. Although this is a struggle for all leaders, it is especially prevalent among freshman leaders. Comparison will only direct a leader into one of two places... 1) pride because they see themselves as better than the rest... 2) false humility because they see themselves less than the rest. Both are deadly. An emerging leader must center themselves and become comfortable in their own skin. It is necessary to trust the talents, experiences, and relationships they have acquired. Personal self-awareness is vital to achieving their goals.

Accomplished leaders still face the same battle. They deal with the comparison trap every day as well. Those who have learned to manage it can be a great help to developing leaders. Here again, their experiences are the catalyst to give aid to a defeated young leader. What self-talk did they create to settle themselves? How do they navigate the relationships in any given room? Why do they avoid certain environments? These men and women have felt the pain of rejection yet managed to grow. They have even abused their own authority to gain control over their adversaries, and yet tasted the sting of being humbled as well. The admission of their current struggle will help emerging leaders see that they are not alone in the fight.

2. **Change**. Change is rarely pleasant but always necessary. It is the path toward uncertainty. Every leader will navigate a season of change. Inherent in change is pain. All leadership will encounter the pain of change because leaders are a catalyst for progress. Young leaders are not experienced with transitions, resulting in simultaneous positive and negative outcomes. The sting that change can bring seeks to devour the courage of young leaders. The pain of change can stop any leader in their tracks. Emerging leaders should become comfortable with an environment of change. Nothing progresses without change. Improvement requires change. A leader who becomes inflexible will eventually break. Think about life itself without change. It dies. A developing leader will do well for themselves if they embrace change as a part of life early in their leadership progression.

Many times established leaders are leading change. How they model that process will be influential in the development of up and coming leaders. Leadership is more caught than taught. Experienced leaders who push change with authority, force, or position will train emerging leaders to control change. They will develop an inner tension that sees any resistance to change as a threat. Some tenured leaders surrender the responsibility for change to subordinates. Their leadership model is to stay away from anything controversial. Young leaders pick this up. When it's their time to address needed adjustments, they fear the accountability and possible repercussions. Established leaders should teach young leaders to find the "why" of change so they can approach it with confidence.

3. **Conflict.** Conflict comes with the leadership package. Someone will disagree. Politics will come into play. Undermining will take place in the hallway. Leaders cannot avoid conflict. Conflict is a heart issue. An apprentice leader would do themselves a great service by mastering the art of conflict. Their people skills and communication skills will serve them well in a climate of conflict. An emerging leader must learn to keep conflict at a distance. Not in the sense of avoiding it, but rather making sure it doesn't become personal. When it becomes personal they open up the emotional realm which normally escalates the issue. Conflict resolution is a learned skill. The earlier a young leader masters these skills, the sooner they will develop the relational equity necessary to move forward.

Established leaders have normally fought their fair share of relational battles. Not all have mastered conflict resolution. However, those who have become a gold mine of leadership wealth to young leaders. The art of peacemaking can be taught. Seasoned leaders who pass this skill on to the growing leaders under them create a culture of honor and respect. Conflict resolution requires humility. Humility can be modeled. Wise and competent leaders who model this attitude build skilled negotiators. An emerging leader cannot always choose their leaders, but when it is possible they should look for mentors with a reputation for bringing unity out of conflict.

<u>Making it Real</u>:

I have always led from a team mindset. It just makes sense for the best outcome. There is a price to pay and pain that comes with leading teams. When I was a novice leader I found myself planting a church. This was long before what church planting is today. I had no dream team that wanted to go with me. It was me, my family, a visiting couple who agreed to come lead worship and a visiting family of four our first Sunday. We began to build from there and soon had over 100 people gathering. We purchased land, built a building and seemed to be on a roll. That is when the scaffolding (the people who join and commit to be lifers) began to crumble. I was shocked. We were in this together. We were a growing family. We were friends and co-laborers for the Kingdom of God. One particular person whom I had entrusted with leadership began to demonstrate an attitude (for example when I stood to preach the person would turn their chair around and look out the window). Didn't they remember the nights I had spent helping them through marriage issues. What about the remodeling of their home and the hours I spent hanging drywall, putting up trim, and painting? All forgotten because they were offended over an offering I had given to a guest speaker. A wise and experienced leader saved me. His sound advice gave me the permission to release the church. The couple who had visited the first Sunday were from the area, bible school graduates, and had pastor's hearts. We set them in as Lead Pastors and we returned home. We were burnt out, crushed in spirit, and felt like failures. But I am here to tell you that those three years have been a reference to many of the leadership lessons, values, and wisdom that we pass on today.

So what is to be learned from my story?

1. I did not have an active coach, mentor, or oversight in my life to guide me through some of the leadership challenges along the way.
2. It is easier to give a title than to take one away.
3. Empowerment is essential but the timing is critical.
4. Family should never be a sacrificial offering to advance the mission.
5. Never promote a person's gift over their character.
6. Clearly defined expectations and job descriptions for every team member.

Emerging Leader Action Items:

1. Purchase the book, StrengthFinder 2.0 by Tom Rath. Once you identify your top five strengths, make a list of the strengths you would need in other team members to have a strong team.
2. Identify two or three areas where you struggle the most with comparison. Now ask yourself why that triggers you to think more of yourself or less of yourself.
3. Write down two ways how you could improve your relationship with the team you lead or the team you serve over the next six weeks.

Experienced Leader Action Items:

1. Take an honest inventory of your fears. Write them down.
2. What is the legacy you want to leave…. Your family? Your team? Your epitaph?

3. Write down and describe what you consider to be your greatest leadership strength. Now record three ways that quality was shaped and developed by people, experiences, or education. Commit to share that with three emerging leaders over the next three months.

> The greatest potential of any leader will only be realized by understanding that they need others to attain it.

Remember:

- ○ Solo leaders are restricted by their own limitations. They are their own leadership lid.
- ○ No leader is immune to the pain of leadership.
- ○ Attitudes impact every relationship
- ○ Trust must be built at all levels for the team to attain maximum proficiency.

FOUR

Tensions & Offenses

IT IS ESSENTIAL FOR GROWING LEADERS TO NAVIGATE TEAM TENSIONS

Emerging Leaders can have an impact if _empowered_ to do so! However, there are some principles concerning managing dynamic tensions and relational offenses that developing leaders must comprehend before moving forward. These are critical for them to gain the opportunities that they are expecting. Once novice leaders master these dynamics they will unlock favor and unleash exponential growth.

Conflict is Good! Not necessarily pleasant or cherished but good, nonetheless. Prospective leaders have to become comfortable with disagreement among team members. They should even encourage it. Young leaders, however, face the challenge of being insecure. Tension demands confidence. When there is stress in the room a nervous leader will kill the opportunity for creative solutions to surface. The writer of Proverbs puts it into perspective with this observation; "Just as iron sharpens iron, friends sharpen the minds of each other." When iron clashes with iron, sparks fly. Strong leaders will compete for their perspective to be heard and considered. Insecure leaders are set back by that type of aggressive behavior and tend to either succumb to the strongest voice in the room or shut down the conversation. Growing leaders need to understand that on the other side of the conflict are the best solutions, creative ideas, and complete buy-in.

Tension demands
confidence.

Proven leaders know the benefits of dynamic tension among team members. Following are a few of those advantages.

➜ _The reality is that not everyone sees problems and opportunities through the same lens._ Life shapes each person differently: from family culture to positive/negative experiences. Together they give each individual a separate viewpoint which can be very valuable to the organization. The aggressive leader who refuses to yield their perspective or let go of their solution(s) will be viewed as intolerant and egotistical, thereby shutting down the opportunity to collaborate with others for the highest ideals and strategies. The reserved leader will need to be coaxed into the conversation in order to draw out their reflective and well thought out perspectives. Diversity of thought, opposing viewpoints, and contrasting solutions lie underneath the surface of every team and a great leader seeks to uncover each of them. Team is about bringing all the dynamics in the room to a unified consensus of thought that is discovered through managing personnel tensions.

→ *It's in the clash of two opposing ideas that truth, best practices, and even personal growth can emerge.* There is always more than one way to get the job done. However, the best solution can be lost unless the proponent of that idea is invited to discuss it, without feeling threatened or demeaned. Leaders who create environments for honest and vulnerable conversations will lead teams to their highest capacity. They build an atmosphere that releases truth because it is a safe place to unpack ideas. If a leader's tendency is to shoot down suggestions or mock them, the team will remain silent, waiting for orders. A great leader will set the table by asking good questions and affirming participation. They read the room, looking for the tensions that can lead the team into meaningful conflict. They hold team members accountable to build a culture of honor and respect. They refuse to allow a member to leave the room without their voice being heard. Team is about everyone in the room, which can only be valued when egos are checked at the door.

→ Conflict resolution principles should be applied when tension is present, but the main point here is that contention between more than one idea can be revelatory to all. When opposing viewpoints are welcomed they can knock the blinders off and allow for a broader perspective. There have been many "ah hah" moments in collaborative conversations. Leaders should never allow conflict to silence the pathway to discovery. This is especially true in tenured organizations or teams that don't realize that tunnel vision has developed and they are blind to it. All teams have a tendency to get in a rut. All leaders face the difficulty of becoming comfortable with the status quo. The way out is conflicting ideals. Many times this can only come about by bringing in an outside consultant with no stake in the game. The key is to bring in a consultant whose resume is not built upon rigid techniques. The team needs someone who will listen, ask penetrating questions, create tension, and then get out of the way. Team is about collaborative discovery without fear.

➜ *The dynamic tension in disagreement can be a catalyst for character development.* Character flaws get exposed in tension. A great leader will allow conflict to expose ulterior motives, conflicting values, and detrimental arrogance so individual growth can occur. Without personal character development team unity will never reach its maximum. In his book, *Integrity*, Dr Henry Cloud gives a great definition of what character means in this context: "Character = the ability to meet the demands of reality." Leaders have to be committed to the development of their team. Every team member comes into the organization with some type of personal baggage, some aspect of a character flaw, some unseen personality quirk, or some preconceived expectations or ideas. Everyone on the team has room for growth including the leader. Pressure, tension, and conflict expose these idiosyncrasies. It is critical that these issues do not go unchecked or be overlooked by the leader. Team chemistry will be destroyed overnight when accountability is inconsistent. Leaders who call teammates out without a platform of reconciliation or path to improvement will create a culture of fear. Others who overlook the toxic actions of a member will empower an atmosphere of jealousy, strife, and gossip. Team is about unity that grows when the leader and the team are committed to healthy accountability and personal development.

> Leaders should never allow conflict to silence the pathway to discovery.

IT IS ESSENTIAL FOR AN EMERGING LEADER TO CAPITALIZE ON PERSONAL OFFENSES

Never Waste a Good Offense! The world is full of imperfect people. People can be misunderstood or they can deliberately manipulate. They have cultural differences, personality quirks, conflicting core beliefs, and values that don't align with others. People come from backgrounds that contain relational wounds, emotional hurts, and consequences of poor choices.

Given these human discrepancies, at some point a person will experience a personal offense. The offense may be self-imposed or may be brutally inflicted by someone they trusted. There is no way out of this life without an offense being experienced. However, offenses can be opportunities in disguise. They can be beneficial when the person gets on the other side of it. The challenge is to see how the leader can benefit from the offense.

OFFENSE IS AN OPPORTUNITY!

Leaders cannot afford to wear their feelings lightly. Leaders are on the top and therefore the focus of judgement and subject to criticism. Seasoned leaders have endured and hopefully grown through these personal attacks. Leadership is pain. Pain is experienced when aggressive assaults are made personal either by the attacker or the leader who is the recipient.

Here are a few perspectives that veterans can teach their young leaders.

An opportunity for personal growth.... When you outlive your critics by thriving on the truth behind what was said or assumed! Truth is what every leader needs in order to overcome blind spots. The discovery of truth can be found in the pain of taking things too personal. Pain causes one to look in the mirror through a different lens. It awakens the recipient to perform a different evaluation of their motives, their skill sets, their position, or their self-esteem. Pride will say the offense has no validity. It tries to bury the pain and avoid any truth that might be present. Anger will strike out at the offender and never examine their actions or re-evaluate their words. Unforgiveness will lock the leader into a never-ending attachment to the offense and offender. They fail to seize any opportunity for growth that might be present in order to plot their revenge. Personal growth occurs when the leader will breathe and allow for an alternate truth to be considered. They engage in self-examination. They invite others to speak into the offense. They humble themselves and embrace a teachable spirit. They open themselves to correction, to discipline, and to change. The opportunity for personal growth can only be achieved when the leaders seek out truth.

> Offenses can be opportunities in disguise.

An opportunity to solve problems.... When the leader refuses to see opposing ideas as threats to their identity! The leader's identity is not in the contribution they bring to the team, but in their ability to be teachable and growth oriented. Moving past being offended and defending their cause can expose them to a world they may never have ventured to discover. Problems are a gift when leaders allow others to speak freely. Yes, it opens them up to become a live target for criticism or disagreement. But, on the other side of any offense that may be incurred, there are solutions that appear like low hanging fruit on a tree. Title oriented leaders will resist any suggested **solutions** that contradict their position. Insecure leaders will shoot holes in **solutions** that oppose their strategic plans. Dominant leaders will demean any **solutions** brought up by their team and force their perspective in the guise of delegation. So, problems either go unsolved or they are met with minimal impact simply because the leader was offended. The opportunity to bring real solutions to the table requires the leader to bring their personal ego in check.

An opportunity to build a team.... When you encourage debate for the sake of discovery and purpose! A team emerges because every player is discovered, valued, and positioned where they can flourish. The leader that wears their offense in public suppresses the potential resident within their team. Easily offended leaders tend to build a culture of fear that discredits the concept of team. Team members refuse to participate because the temperamental leader crushes them rather than celebrates them. When a leader can handle alternative viewpoints which are allowed and even welcomed, they lay the foundation for a healthy team. Debates, disagreements, disputes that are harnessed by an unoffendable leader can produce the framework necessary for strong partnerships. On the backside of hearty relational conflict lies the discovery of strong alliances that allow for substantive solutions. The possibility of offense remains but the wise leader will ask the right questions to manage the tension, while empowering the team to sustain its momentum. Collaboration, cooperation, and coordination exists when the participants can trust the leader to control the tension. The complete capacity of the team will be realized when the leader leverages their personal offense as fuel for inclusivity rather than personal isolation.

An opportunity to see the future.... When you open yourself to see what's beyond reconciliation! No one person can predict the outcome of today's decisions. A decision to reconcile may unlock the relational equity needed to revive momentum. They reconcile differences to invite the wisdom of others to the table to get their company moving. Leaders who refuse to burn bridges build a reservoir of relationships that could unlock future doorways and opportunities. Tomorrow is an unknown entity. Leaders minimize future mistakes by being vulnerable and refusing to be the only expert in the room! They understand that one perspective at the table could unveil truth and reveal the way forward. They value relationships over results because in the long run relationships are required to sustain results. Cutting someone off because they seem to be running against the grain could prove fatal. The restorative and relational leader gains a great advantage to acquire the future success they desire to achieve.

→ A 360° plan is hammered out when all voices on the team are heard

Leaders minimize future mistakes by refusing to be the only expert in the room!

Making it Real:

I walked into the green room for the pre-conference meeting. The week prior had been a great week. The department I was leading had made significant strides forward. We were seeing the impact of our efforts and vision taking shape. I was excited for the future and I had entered the green room feeling the euphoria of success. After the meeting, our senior leader asked me to stay behind. I was sure that he wanted to compliment our progress. That was not the case. I found myself being reprimanded for using an outside organization and representing their values. That was painful enough. But, the nail through my heart was when he said, "Bobby you don't work for them, you work for me." Yes sir.

I left that room offended. Why didn't he see all the good that had come from our partnership with that organization? After all, we supported them financially. Besides, his representation of my position was unfounded and based solely on one email salutation. I was defending my actions to myself and hurt by the straightforwardness of his rebuke.

He was right though. I did work for him. I was employed to assist the mission of that organization and represent the culture he had established. My "rights" were subjugated to his authority and the company's employee handbook. My assignment was to lead my team and my department with integrity while honoring the leadership over me.

So what is to be learned from my story?

1. No human interaction is without conflict. How you respond to it matters.
2. Honor is given as much as it is earned.
3. My offense caused me to examine my motive, my commitment to the organization, and my values. Truth became my best friend.

4. If you are faithful under another person's leadership, you will advance and be given your own leadership platform.

> * I was promoted from the Executive Leadership to the Senior Leadership of that organization a couple of years following this incident.

Emerging Leader Action Items:
1. Purchase the book, Integrity, by Dr. Henry Cloud.
2. Write yourself a 500-word document on the most difficult conflict you've encountered in leadership and define what you character trait it addressed.
3. Develop a survey to solicit feedback on how you handle conflict. Now ask three peers and one oversight to complete it. Survey Monkey is a good tool to use.

Established Leader Action Items:
1. Gather a group of leaders in a non-threatening space (preferably outside the office or work environment) and share how you navigated some difficult conflicts on your way to becoming a better leader.
2. Allow the group the opportunity to ask questions.
3. Take the risk to make yourself vulnerable and share your defeats, as well as, your victories.

Remember:
- A great leader will set the table by asking good questions and affirming participation.
- The reality is that not everyone sees problems and opportunities through the same lens.
- Team is about unity that grows when the leader and the team are committed to healthy accountability and personal development.
- The opportunity to bring real solutions to the table requires the leader to bring their personal ego in check.
- Character flaws get exposed in tension.

TENSIONS & OFFENSES

FIVE

Discipline & Lifestyle

◄————————————————►

IT IS ESSENTIAL FOR EMERGING LEADERS TO DISCIPLINE THEIR LIFESTYLES!

Every Emerging Leader must master these four disciplines. Finances, Time Management, Health (spiritual, physical), and Growth. Since much has been written on each of these topics, the focus here will mostly be on the **why** and only offer a few suggestions on the **how**. Needless to say, history is full of great leaders and potentially great leaders who have taken a headlong plunge into the abyss. Their failures leave behind wounded humanity and put a black eye on the name of Christianity. Most of these fallen men and women started out with pure intentions and a passion to accomplish great things. They were emerging leaders who failed to consider Paul's exhortation to a growing leader named Timothy: **1 Timothy 4:16, "Keep a close watch on how you live and on your teaching. Stay true to what is right for the sake of your own salvation and the salvation of those who hear you."**

Finances.

Because this book is written from a biblical worldview, the Bible must be considered on this topic. Why financial discipline? Jesus answered the why of financial discretion when he made the statement, "Wherever your treasure is, there the desires of your heart will also be." Matthew 6:21 (NLT) The heart of any person is revealed by their financial investments. So when scripture speaks to the battle between mammon (riches) and God, the focus is on the heart.

- Robert Morris, in his book The Blessed Life, makes the point clear when he writes, "Mammon is the spirit that rests on money. Did you know that all money has a spirit on it? It either has the Spirit of God on it, or the spirit of Mammon."
- Emerging leaders will break the spirit of Mammon and keep their hearts focused on God by building the disciplines of generosity and stewardship.
- When the discipline of putting God first in financial matters becomes a lifestyle, these young leaders will begin to live free of the entrapments that the pursuit of riches seem to offer.
- Does this mean a vow of poverty? By no means! Paul encouraged the church at Corinth with these words of financial provision regarding their mission and work, "And God is able to bless you abundantly, so that in all things at all times, having all that you need, you will abound in every good work." 2 Corinthians 9:8 (NIV)

Why financial discipline?
- It puts full trust in God.
- It is a stabilizer for marriages.
- It provides freedom from money worries.

- It creates a margin for generosity.
- This list is endless.... So fill in the blank.... It

_____ .

Lastly, consider the fact that over 2,000 verses in scripture speak to the subject of money and possessions. Also, nearly half of the parables that Jesus spoke were about money. These two considerations alone speak to the reality that how money is handled is important. Reflect on it one more time, "The place where your treasure is, is the place you will most want to be, and end up being." Matthew 6:21 (MSG)

IT IS ESSENTIAL FOR EMERGING LEADERS TO DISCIPLINE THEIR LIFESTYLES!

Senior leaders take the risk! Many emerging leaders grew up without a father or mother who taught them about finances. Most never took an economics class or have any formal education regarding stewardship. TAKE THE RISK! Probe into the personal lives of those you lead. Help them break free from the money weight that is destroying their dreams, straining their marriages, or making them susceptible to schemes to get wealthy quickly. So many are drowning under student loans. Others have been unable to resist the "get in now on credit" and have maxed their credit balances. Still others spend everything they have and live paycheck to paycheck.

Why get involved? Because when these young leaders have stability in their finances, they will be less likely to embezzle funds, misuse company credit cards, or steal. Here are a few suggestions how to bridge this important subject with young leaders.

1. Set up a relational oversight system. This is a specific oversight meeting for building relational equity. It consists of a conversation about the employees dreams for the future, about the welfare of their family, about the status of their health, and about any stress points in their lives. Here the discussion of finances can easily be entered into. It is recommended that this occur at least once a month.

2. Have an opt out financial seminar or curriculum offered to all employees. Here budgeting can be taught. The emerging leader can also learn how to invest and establish a retirement plan.

3. Be willing to provide crisis assistance whenever possible.

4. Have quarterly round tables where you invite financial specialists in for specific topics. This will help the individual as well as help them oversee department budgets.

5. Believe your efforts will pay off for the individual and the company!

Time Management

Time is our greatest resource. There are only 24 hours in a day and every person only has one life to live. No one can rewind time. Once it is lived, it is gone. So it is necessary for a developing leader to manage their time well. Again, there are countless time management books with a variety of systems that work. The challenge is managing self in the midst of managing time.

- Self says, "This is only a season." When the reality is that it is "only a season" that has followed on the heels of another "only a season" and burnout is just around the corner.
- Self believes that if it does more, works harder, and spends more time doing it, productivity will increase and the outcomes will be better. Yet many studies and countless research have proven that longer and harder are not the healthiest or best solutions.

An up-and-coming leader must be cognizant that time will only be managed to the level of truthful self-management. For example: vacation cannot be a 35-40% disconnect from work and 60-65% involvement with texting, emails, phone calls, and video conferences. Vacation is time managed to rest, to let the family be the focus, or to do anything else but engage in work.

> Time is our greatest resource.

There is a deception that self is a superhero who can take on more clients, burn the midnight oil, work more hours, and never say no to new opportunities. The truth is that a leader who cannot manage themselves well will never manage their time well. **Being on top of time management means being on top of self-awareness.**

Time management is an endless war. Leaders know only so much time exists to accomplish their goals. The juggle between work, family, hobbies, friendships, events, and dreams is never ending. There is help. It is found in the wisdom of the Proverbs, "Trust in the Lord with all your heart; do not depend on your own understanding. Seek His will in all you do, and He will show you which path to take." Proverbs 3:5,6 (NLT)

<u>Established Leaders You Can Make a Difference</u>! When starting the leadership journey there is a desire to make an impression! The emerging leader puts their head down and goes for it. However, many developing leaders have young families. They are juggling work, family, marriage, kids extracurricular activities, extended family functions, religious participation, and a social life. They are going 24/7/365 and many times without regard to the emotional, physical, and mental wear and tear because they are young.

YOU CAN MAKE A DIFFERENCE! Here again begs the question, why help? A tired work force is less productive. More job-related accidents are likely due to fatigue. Creativity is stifled because that space has been used up. Tension and fighting occur more often in a weary team. Maybe these suggestions will aid in the effort to assist these up and coming women and men.

1. Many today are offering a flexible work schedule allowing team members to plan their work hours themselves within certain parameters.
2. Another option being extended to the present workforce is the ability to work from home. This allows employees to juggle family demands more efficiently while continuing to meet the demands of their job description.
3. Minimize vacation roll over. Encourage emerging leaders to take vacations that disconnect them from the company.
4. Make sure the workforce has the ability to take a minimum of one day but preferably two days off each week.
5. Model the balance between work and family.
6. Bring in time management consultants to educate the team about their workspace, about how to create time saving processes, and about how they should value their time.
7. Have realistic work expectations and minimize seasonal pushes where it's all hands on deck to meet crisis deadlines.

Personal & Spiritual Health

This will not be a health and wellness tirade. However, there is a strong case for approaching this topic with a sober and straight forward disposition. Growing leaders are usually young and vibrant. They are usually in sound physical condition and possess a strong mental temperament. These energetic leaders set off to conquer the world. They climb the ladder of success relatively quickly. The higher they climb the less oxygen there is in the atmosphere. As they ascend they find themselves more alone than in the beginning. Each new altitude presents weightier responsibilities and pressures. They find themselves fatigued more often. Their sleep evades them. They can't turn off their thoughts. Emotionally they are on edge. The relationships they do have are strained. Why?

- They chose caffeine and other stimulants over a healthy six - eight hours of sleep.
- They chose an extra hour or two at work over a round of golf or a relaxing evening at home.
- They chose to be in charge instead of delegating to and empowering others.
- They chose eating on the run over well balanced meals.
- They chose to make work their identity over being secure in themselves.
- They chose the pursuit of title and success over significant relationships.
- They chose a life of stress over seasons of rest.
- They chose loose living over having spiritual pursuits.

Each choice eroded their physical stamina. Each decision added weight that took a toll on their emotional well-being. Each broken relationship drove them deeper into their fixation on fame and fortune. Each integral breach sent them into shame and guilt.

Realistically this is not everyone who takes on leadership. But it does paint the picture for the need of a balanced lifestyle. For the record, a balanced lifestyle does not mean everything is always set to even keel. A healthy lifestyle is achieved when everything is truthfully addressed to bring about moderate swings over extreme changes. Moderation is not the lack of aggression or passion but the ability to let things adjust and stabilize before moving forward. Personal health is simply being honest about the places that need attention so that maximum potential is realized.

Emerging leaders will set the foundation for addressing their overall health in their early years. If bad habits are excused and allowed, they are harder to break. Young leaders would be wise to build their cultural values around a commitment to holistic health.

> Being on top of time
> management means being
> on top of self-awareness.

When it comes to spiritual health the formula is simple. Spend time with God. Read and meditate on His word. Seek His current perspective. Know the Holy Spirit's directives for today. These truths are poured into every Christian leader from the time they begin a relationship with God. Volumes of books have been written to reveal the spiritual power and influence acquired through daily communion with Jesus. Thousands, no millions, of sermons exhort congregations to build a spiritual formation which makes room for a consistent relationship with God. Yet, there seems to be a disconnect between a devout Christian and their work. Dualism is a belief that all spiritual life must be separated from the world of human interaction, especially when it comes to work. The question that surfaces in a dualistic environment is "Can spiritual leaders exist in the marketplace?" So spiritual life is lived on Sunday, and the rest of the week life is experienced through the constraints of humanism. Leadership decisions are made in business every day without regard to a biblical worldview. Young leaders need to crucify the dualistic pull on their lives.

- Think of Joseph. His story is about the calling to administrate a kingdom.
- Elijah was able to speak to the king's distress.
- Jesus even taught professional fishermen how to fish!

Why address a leader's spiritual health? Because it is the one thing that empowers them to be effective in their leadership. Spiritually healthy leaders can offer the marketplace insights that can only be gained through a life of faith. Keeping a strong relationship with the King opens opportunity for discernment that reveals ulterior motives, spirit-led strategic planning, revelations that solve problems, prophetic forecasts that protect resources, and anointed vision casting.

Seasoned Leaders Ask How You Help! Health is an ongoing issue. It can involve so many factors that there isn't a "one size fits all" solution. Some health problems are self-inflicted and some blindside a person. Factors like stress, family difficulties, money problems, broken relationships, mental issues, and the list goes on all impact the well-being of an individual. So how does a veteran leader help an emerging leader stay healthy? Consider the following:

1. Knowing someone cares goes a long way. Just asking the question sincerely, "How are you doing?"

2. Not having all the answers but showing compassion will make a difference. The statement, "I am so sorry!" delivered with deep empathy can impact the heart and soul.

3. Sharing your personal story. "This may or may not apply but, this is what I went through and this is how I got through it!"

4. Prayer. "I'm a praying person... would you mind if I prayed for you?"

<u>Growth</u>

The curse of experience is the tendency to believe one has arrived. When aging leaders take on the attitude of "been there, done that," they immediately move toward becoming obsolete. While young leaders enter the field eager to learn, they will do well for themselves to make it a conviction to never stop growing in knowledge, skills, and wisdom. The internet is full of pathways for growth and development. Libraries hold wisdom from ages past and offer opportunities for leaders to advance. However, much like time management, leaders only grow to the level of self-discipline.

Development does not come through osmosis or wishful thinking. **Every growing leader is a learning leader**. When a leader is always the smartest person in the room, they have capped their potential for advancement. **When a leader is not growing they are regressing.**

Young leaders must find their rhythm for growth and establish disciplines that create space for learning. Reading, listening to the wisdom of others, researching for answers, trying new things, attending seminars, taking advantage of company leadership development curriculum, teaching and training others, are all opportunities for those hungry to learn. Learning equips the leader to help others.

- Growing in knowledge and wisdom make the leader valuable because they can more readily solve problems.
- Honing their strengths establishes the leader as an expert in their field. Learning leaders are change agents.
- They are making others around them better, and they reinforce a culture of excellence.

When it comes to spiritual health the formula is simple. Spend time with God. Read and meditate on His word. Seek His current perspective. Know the Holy Spirit's directives for today.

Experienced Leader You Know What It Takes! Every successful leader understands the importance of learning. Look at the journey of any top leader and you will see a path of learning that parallels their advancement. Knowledge solves problems. Solving problems creates a sought-after leader. An emerging leader has an insatiable desire to learn…. YOU KNOW WHAT IT TAKES! Consider…

1. Directing novices to the right resources for growth.
2. Connecting emerging leaders to other mentors in your field.
3. Spending personal time one on one for open Q & A.

4. Making opportunities for advanced education.
5. Developing a culture of learning.

Both emerging leaders and established leaders must address these disciplines as a lifestyle not a process. It's in the process of living that each discipline comes alive and bears fruit. Life ebbs and flows with each new season bringing challenges and opportunities. It is within this flux that a lifetime is lived. It is imperative to recall Paul's exhortation to a growing leader named Timothy: 1 Timothy 4:16 "Keep a close watch on how you live and on your teaching. Stay true to what is right for the sake of your own salvation and the salvation of those who hear you."

Making it Real:

In 1993 I joined a growing nonprofit led by one of the most disciplined individuals I have ever met. Some called him "The Clock." His life was lived like a fine Swiss watch with calibrated precision. He was up every morning at 5am preparing himself mentally, spiritually, and physically for the day ahead. He regimented his weekly office routines with staff and key leaders. He was an avid outdoorsman with weekend get-aways on the farm, on the lake fishing, or in the woods hunting. He was widely read and continually educating himself in his professional skills, in finance, and in cultural trends. The organization mirrored his disciplines with a consistency seen in growth, in influence, in expansion, and in leadership development. When I left thirteen years later the nonprofit had over 7,000 participants reflecting an annual growth rate of 20% per year. We had expanded to three local campuses and multiplied by sending thirteen leaders and start ups throughout the state. The main campus grew from an 85,000 square foot complex to over 300,000 square feet under roof. The financial margins were such that we were able to give support to other nonprofits of roughly a million dollars per year. This leader protected the culture, refused to be swayed by trending nuances, held the team accountable to the mission and values of the organization, and empowered those around him to pursue their dreams.

So what is to be learned from my story?

1. Leaders are focused.
2. Disciplines give strength to the present and posture us for future success.
3. Your lifestyle is the lid on your future potential.

4. The ripple effect of consistency can reach farther than you may ever imagine.

Emerging Leaders Action Items:

1. Rate your discipline and consistency in each area that was discussed in the chapter. Scale your rating: 1-10 but leave out the 7

2. Make a list of people who can help you grow in each area.... Even if you rated a 9.

3. Schedule a one on one meeting and draw on their wisdom.

Established Leaders Action Items:

1. Read John Maxwell's book, "The Leader's Greatest Return."

2. Read back through the action items we suggested in this chapter.

3. Highlight the ones that you can implement with your team or mentee.

Remember:

- Being on top of time management means being on top of self-awareness.

- Moderation is not the lack of aggression or passion but the ability to let things adjust and stabilize before moving forward.

- The curse of experience is the tendency to believe one has arrived.

- Every growing leader is a learning leader. When a leader is not growing they are regressing.

DISCIPLINE & LIFESTYLE

SIX

F-Words

<hr>

IT IS ESSENTIAL FOR EMERGING LEADERS TO AVOID F-WORDS

Emerging Leaders can stumble if they don't address the F-Words! Every leader is challenged by failure, fatigue, fear, and fraud. However, young leaders are especially susceptible to the traps of these F-Words. Many good leaders have fallen out of the race because failure defined them, fatigue wore them down, fear paralyzed them, and fraud compromised their integrity. Here are some insights that may help.

→ **Failure** is really more of a question than a statement. Failure asks, do you have the tenacity to get back up and try again? It inquires whether or not the leader will die in perfectionism or awaken to learning. Failure is looking for an answer. How will the leader react to a setback? Can they turn obstacles into opportunities? Will a defeat turn into a step toward success or will it derail the leader into someone who lives in mediocrity? Failure wants to know. It wants to know if it can define the leader's identity. It wants to uncover the stress point that causes the leader to collapse. Failure wants to discover if it can paralyze the leader's potential. It reminds the leader of past failures and prophecies the same results. Failure is ruthless. It pours out condemnation. It heaps on shame. It shouts, "Worthless!" It never lets up. Failure calls upon the comparison trap to strengthen its grip on the leader's faults. It summons voices of the past that declared; "You will never amount to anything!" "You screw up everything you touch!" "You can't do anything right!" Failure is an enemy. Failure is always chasing, always reminding, always haunting young leaders to defeat them before they can get started.

However, handled correctly, failure can become the fuel for a favorable outcome. It doesn't have to be the final word! Failure can be overcome. Listen to the insights of these seasoned leaders:

➜ Mark Batterson said, "Success is really well-managed failure."
➜ John Maxwell wrote, "Failure is an essential step in the cycle of success."
➜ Craig Groeschel stated, "If something doesn't challenge you -- it won't change you."

Mistakes, mishaps, defeat, collapse, and even catastrophe are inevitable in the life of anyone willing to lead. Emerging leaders can only reach their full potential by understanding that to succeed, one has to be willing to fail. Success and failure lie on the other side of taking a risk, entering uncharted water, and the willingness to take on new challenges. Tragedies can become triumphs only by confronting the dread of failing again. Someone once noted that a person who never made a mistake never made anything. Young leaders will do well for themselves to develop the courage to take on new ventures without letting failures become fatal. They have to learn to get back up. They have to take on failure's assaults by sustaining the faith and confidence to try again.

> Mistakes, mishaps, defeat, collapse, and even catastrophe are inevitable in the life of anyone willing to lead.

Failure can be enabled by fatigue.

→ **Fatigue** is subtle. It creeps in and then erupts. It is almost always sloughed off and excused. Fatigue will erode the fibers of a leader's soul, stamina, and skills. The process of this illness is slow but deliberate. It masks itself in deadlines, busyness, seasons, and productivity. The lie is embedded in the notion that if one does more than everyone else, does it longer than anyone else, and does it faster than anyone else then success is inevitable. Energy, vigor, and vitality are lost as a person engaged in such a mindset grows tired, sluggish, and eventually exhausted. Some believe that fatigue is a contributing factor in 70% of workplace accidents. It's most common consequences are a lack of concentration, emotional upheaval, impaired judgement, and poor communication. Fatigue can be caused by low immune systems and other physical ailments. However, much of the fatigue in today's culture is the result of never being able to shut down. Cell phones, emails, social media, business, family, online purchasing, workload, special activities.... And the list goes on and on. The information overload is enough in itself to tire any normal person. Emerging leaders want to prove themselves. They pump themselves full of energy drinks and/or caffeine as they hit the day running. The drive to make a difference, the push to impress their oversight, or the pressure to compete with their peers, all set them up for the path to fatigue. Leaders are by nature self-starters, entrepreneurial, and aggressive. They run hard to get things accomplished. Nothing wrong with that until the energy levels are depleted.

Fatigue is avoidable.

Fatigue is avoidable. A growing leader needs to pay attention when they begin to hear themselves say things like:

→ "I'm going to work late tonight,"
→ "Honey we are just in a season,"
→ A late night turns into "I'll be working late all week."

→ A season begins to be followed immediately by another season.

These are the paving stones for a road called **FATIGUE**. It's only a matter of time.... the stress builds, the anger manifests, the impatience sets in, and the physical stamina wanes. Fatigue has now mastered its subject! Don't misunderstand. Hard work is ok. Seasons do come. Progress has to be made. But the approach can make all the difference in the world.

Here are a few suggestions from seasoned leaders:

→ **make sure your day has built in breaks**
Daily breaks need to be more than a walk to the coffee pot and back to your desk. Go outside, get some fresh air, take a walk to another side of the building, call someone for a conversation that is not work related; somehow disengage from the mental and physical work of the day. Put it in your calendar as an appointment. Inform all support staff that there are no interruptions allowed unless its family or a life and death crisis. Then utilize the time... not to catch up on projects... use it to take a power nap, listen to some relaxing music, or take a drive. A daily break is a break... it doesn't have to be long but it does have to be purposeful.

→ **build a full day of rest into your weekly schedule**
When you take a day off, take a day off. If needed, turn the phone off. Refuse work related activity. Do anything but work! Find an activity that relates to the area of rest that is needed. For example: if the need is for some relational connection then plan a day with friends. Some days may need to be filled with naps, physical exercise, or a walk in the woods to provide

physical and emotional rest. Whatever the need is; physical, mental, emotional, spiritual, or relational, find the disconnect method that meets the corresponding need.

→ take your annual vacation time with minimal rollover

Vacation time is a must! Work will still be there when vacation has ended. Two keys to consider for making vacation a priority. 1) Plan workloads before the vacation begins so that it includes some detox time going into vacation. The goal is to have others accountable and equipped to take on the workload days before leaving the office. This allows for any last-minute questions or needed information to be addressed. Now there is a confidence that everything will have someone responsible during the duration of the vacation. 2) It is also important to have a re-entry plan to re-engage at work. Several days before re-entry check emails for any updates. Do not respond to them. Simply make strategic notes that highlight two or three things that can create solutions. Only make calls that are critical. These calls should be short and to the point. The calls are made in order to alleviate any stress or loss of sleep that a lack of communication could create. Inform the teammate that vacation isn't over and the call is about letting them know there is an awareness the problem exists. Have them outline a plan of action that can be reviewed day one in the office. These two suggestions allow for a true disconnect.

→ honestly evaluate your workload

Fatigue only wins when it is empowered through excuses, poor planning, and the refusal to delegate. A super hero complex or a martyr mentality both feed the idea that "I'm the only one who can do this." So the workload mounts. It becomes all consuming. Longer hours are needed to get it done. More days are required for the project to be completed. Simply because the workload isn't honestly evaluated. This doesn't mean there needs to be a frantic search for a dumping ground to offload work to someone else or hire a new employee. It does mean that honesty has to be applied so that truth can be revealed. That may mean there has to be an admission that there is a need to work smarter not harder. It could also mean that Miss Super Hero can't carry the present load or that Mr Martyr has to relinquish some authority. Whatever the case, workloads can be deceptive because employees normally focus on what they enjoy and procrastinate the undesirable portion of their responsibilities. Many time workers are engaged in activities and responsibilities outside their personal job descriptions because they desire another position, have a need to feel needed, or crave the comradery another department provides. When added things are taken on or when the workload actually is over capacity, they will create unnecessary fatigue which could easily have been avoided.

<u>Along with failure and fatigue, the **FEAR** factor is always nipping at a leader's heels.</u>

→ **FEAR!** The fear of failure, the fear of rejection, the fear of ridicule, the fear of others, the fear of the past, the fear of judgement, the fear of conflict, or the fear of the future. Fear is paralyzing. Fear is a reality. The person that says "I fear nothing" is a liar. Everyone is afraid of something. Fear seeks to put boundaries on potential by capturing its prey with lies, assumptions, and unknowns. Once a leader yields to the influence of fear they become insecure in that area of leadership. Insecure leaders are detrimental. Fear has been acronymed as: False Evidence Appearing Real. Fear is usually based on a presumption that may or may not be reality but to the carrier it becomes their reality... true or not. When fear grips an individual they lose their way. They either begin to control everything around them as much as possible to minimize the fear factor or they begin to withdraw and disconnect in order to protect themselves from the perceived consequences of being engaged. Fearful leaders are usually passive/aggressive. They can implode into a master martyr or explode into an angry taskmaster at any given moment. These leaders build a culture of fear. Teams around them are either wounded servants who fear retribution or highly frustrated individuals silenced by scorn.

➜ Matt Keller drew a stark contrast between a confident and an insecure leader when he made this declaration, "You lead to the proportion of your faith... You control to the proportion of your fear."

➜ There are a couple of great lines from the movie, Coach Carter, that also set this contrast in perspective. "Our deepest fear is not that we are inadequate. Our deepest fear is that we are powerful beyond measure. It's our light, not our darkness, that scares us most. As we are liberated from our own fear, our presence automatically liberates others." So powerful!

<u>Emerging Leaders must learn to navigate away from fear-based decisions</u>. Courage is not the absence of fear. Courage is the willingness to act in spite of the fear. There will always be adversity confronting every endeavor that brings significant results. These are the moments when fearless leaders emerge. They shed the self-doubt, then step into the uncertainty and prevail over their personal anxiety. Fear calls out but faith shouts it down. These leaders remain secure in their decisions. They resolve to work through any unseen difficulties. They are willing to risk failure, to put their reputation on the line, to deal with the ensuing conflicts, and to be vulnerable to scrutiny. Fear is their fuel not their limitation.

> Along with failure
> and fatigue, the
> FEAR factor is
> always nipping at a
> leader's heels.

However, uncontrolled fear can lead to the deadliest and career ending F-Words…… **FRAUD!**

→ **FRAUD!** It's when an emerging leader begins to live the life of deception. Think about it. If a young leader is demoralized by a failure, then tries to recover through a workaholic life resulting in total fatigue, which in turn creates the foundation for fear-based decision making. To mask it all they hide behind a life of compromise. Once a young leader compromises their values, they endanger their ability to lead. There are many developing leaders who never dreamed of being a fraudulent leader. They never started out to become a fraud. Even the word itself was and is repulsive to them. But, they didn't manage expectations. They failed to overcome setbacks. They fell into comparing themselves with their peers. They felt pressure to succeed. Time management eluded them. Financial pressures overcame them. Maybe the need for approval and recognition drove them to the point they stepped across the line of integrity. Frauds are deceptive, manipulative, duplicitous, and fearful. These qualities set them up for a fall. Seasons can come and go when it seems they are getting by with their misdeeds. However, time will reveal their motives and uncover their sins. Some frauds maliciously defraud their company, their co-leaders, and their subordinates. But most found themselves upside down before they realized what had happened. Now they remain ensnared by the fear of discovery.

The pathway to their imprisonment was their negligence to deal with the F-Words in their lives. They chose the pathway of least resistance. They refused the disciplines necessary to anchor their hearts in integrity and wisdom. Excuses and blame shifting became their protection in seasons of failure. Everyone and everything but them caused the breakdown. However, the reality was that because they didn't guard their hearts failure captivated their identity. The fight was on and they had to prove themselves. Work, work, and more work became their new motto for life. Slowly but surely they began to wear themselves out. The stress was more about the work to prove, to cover, to protect than it was about the physical or intellectual labor. Worn and weary they began to plug the holes and gaps with deception, manipulation, and lies. Fatigue now has entry points into every area of their lives. They become short tempered. Exhaustion impacts their decision making with confusion. Empty of energy they start looking for stimulants to keep themselves motivated. Drained, they look for relief from their pain. Panic is experienced for the first time in their lives. Fear begins to dominate every thought. Fear of men. Fear of more failure. Fear of crashing. Fear, fear, and more fear! They need a way out. They need a short-cut to success. They need someone. They need more influence, more money, and more power. The drive is relentless and presses them daily. One morning they wake up and it has all caught up with them. They never dreamed of being in this place. They are broken. Now there are consequences to their fraudulent life. Marriages destroyed. Reputations lost. Innocent lives crushed. For what?

Making it Real:

It hurt. When the news first broke, I refused to believe what I was hearing. But the facts followed. Now we were facing the outcome of a fallen leader. How could he have done this? Why make such a dumb choice? What else had he covered up? Was there really more to the story? The questions kept coming. Some people were downright mean and judgmental. They wanted to go for the jugular. Others were sloppy with grace. They loved the man and didn't want to see him hurt further. We had to manage it and we did not even cause the problem. We had to find the best solution and outcome for the chaos. We had to navigate what restoration might look like in the midst two opposing factions: crucify him or forgive him. It was a mess started by one man's impropriety.

Looking back over the years and being involved in other similar situations it easy to see the progression of the downfalls. The slide begins the minute a leader begins to think more about themself than others around them. Scriptures states that we are drawn into our downfalls by our own lusts (cravings for things outside of moral boundaries). Once the leader legitimizes in their own mind why the actions they are about to take are ok for them, the tipping point happens. Now it becomes a matter of seizing the opportunities that present themselves for the fulfillment of their lusts: greed, sexual appetites, power, or prestige. What sets them up for such pursuits? They started out with pure hearts, noble initiatives, and legitimate desires. But somewhere along the way they began to neglect the basics. They ran too hard. They compared themselves to others. They didn't manage their emotions. They excused themselves from accountability. Whatever the case, they left a destructive pathway behind them for others to navigate. It hurts.

Emerging Leaders Action Items:

1. Purchase and Read, "Leading on Empty," by Wayne Cordeiro
2. Purchase and Read, "Replenish," by Lance Witt
3. Purchase and Read, "Addicted to Busy," by Brady Boyd
4. Now Develop a Teaching / Training that You will Present to Your Team

Established Leaders Action Items:

1. Purchase and Read, "Leading on Empty," by Wayne Cordeiro
2. Purchase and Read, "Replenish," by Lance Witt
3. Purchase and Read, "Addicted to Busy," by Brady Boyd
4. Merge the learnings from these books with your own journey and teach them to a group of emerging leaders.

Remember:

- Failure asks, do you have the tenacity to get back up and try again?
- Failure wants to know. It wants to know if it can define the leader's identity.
- Fatigue will erode the fibers of a leader's soul, stamina, and skills.
- Fear seeks to put boundaries on potential by capturing its prey with lies, assumptions, and unknowns.
- Courage is the willingness to act in spite of the fear.
- No leader started out to live the life of a fraudulent person.

F-WORDS

SEVEN

The "Who" in Your Life is Critical

◄━━━━━━━━━━━━━━━━━━━━━━━━━►

Every leader depends on the relationships in their world. Key relationships are imperative to accomplish anything of significance. King Solomon put it this way, "Whoever walks with the wise will be wise but the companion of fools will be destroyed." Proverbs 13:20. Leaders must realize that "the who" in their life is critical to their success. A young and developing leader would do well to consider four significant relationships.

Peripheral Relationships
A peripheral relationship is one where there is little or no relational equity between the leader and the person being engaged. These relationships are far from insignificant, however. They provide a leader the best unbiased feedback possible. People on the peripheral give leaders important insights into cultural values and pain points. These perceptions could improve delivery systems, communication pieces, marketing strategies, or customer care. For example, if a leader never walks about the office to interact with their staff, they could assume they have a healthy environment of team unity. However, a spontaneous conversation with a staffer could

reveal a needed change in policy or an adjustment in procedures to minimize the schisms that really exist throughout the organization.

Church leadership would do well to develop a variety of peripheral relationships in their community. They say a person who has been a devoted Christian over a year has few, if any, connections outside their church world. Maybe that is why the church is considered to be out of touch.

Now take this into business and government. When leaders disengage from their constituents or customers, they govern or do business from a framework of elitism. Common trends are missed. Feedback is ignored or overlooked. Utilizing case studies and product surveys can provide statistical and general information, however they cannot replace human awareness or exposure. When a young leader touches and feels the community, they come away with a personal experience. Take movies for example. Critics will give their perception of the movie's quality. Yet those who attend can come away with a completely different take on it, simply because of what they personally experienced in the storyline, the cinematography, or the persona of the actors. Emerging leaders should make it a point to consistently touch the peripheral public to stay grounded and relevant.

Ask a seasoned leader! They will undoubtedly be able to recount a time when they happened to "bump into a person." That person opened their eyes to see things from a different perspective. I wonder how many creative ideas were spawned from an inflight conversation with the stranger in the adjoining seat. Others may have encountered someone solving a problem similar to the one that has frustrated them for months. These people were not close friends. They were not hired consultants or personal coaches. Some of the encounters that rocked their worlds were just passers-by. A casual interaction but a life altering exchange. Don't count out those individuals that may seem insignificant. ***They may very well be a Godsend!***

The "Who" in Your Life is Critical

Purposeful Friendships

Friendships are formed on many levels. Work friendships. Neighborhood friendships. Family friendships. People look for community whenever they interact with others. Friendships are categorized by time spent, trust that is built, and vulnerability that is experienced. They fall into categories like casual friends, close friends, and then there are best friends. Leaders find that the more they advance in their leadership the more selective they have to become with their friendships. This is observed even in the life of Jesus Christ. He was accessible to the multitudes but He chose twelve as close friends, and within those He had three that were "best friends." These are the guys He went up to the Mount of Transfiguration with and the men He asked to pray with Him in the Garden of Gethsemane. Friendships next to immediate family have the greatest impact upon a leader's values, worldview, and ethics. Understanding this is important.

Friends are chosen. Because of their impact, they must be chosen wisely. Affinity and familiarity are not enough. Whomever a leader decides to do life with will either open or close doors of opportunity. Leaders set themselves up for success or failure through chosen friendships. This would encompass everyone from team leads to close social companions.

Some great questions for emerging leaders to ask themselves regarding friendships would be:

1. Does this person reinforce my values and worldview?
2. How do my closest friends impact my decisions?
3. Can I advance to the next level of leadership with my current friendships?
4. What friendships do I need to pursue to add value to my life?
5. Are my friends growing and moving forward in their own lives?
6. Will I be better in five years as a result of those around me?

Are these questions self-serving? Yes. Why? Because to realize maximum potential, a leader must seriously consider who they allow into their inner circle. A life of purpose requires purposeful friendships. Does a leader value everyone? They should. But that doesn't mean everyone has intimate access or personal influence in their life. Emerging leaders should give serious consideration regarding purposeful friendships.

How many previous established leaders have fallen? They once were on their game and were heralded by all as significant leaders of their day. But, something happened. These great men and women failed in their friendships. It's not that they didn't have people around them. They did. However, they resisted closeness. They held at bay those who could hold them accountable. When their worlds grew in influence their relationships faded in intimacy. Veteran leaders who have survived the fray of popularity will tell you about the men and women in their corner. Friends who asked the tough questions. Associates that helped them battle pride. Many close relationships that helped them find solutions, solve problems, and enlarge their capacity for leading at a higher level. Proverbs 18:24 " A man who has friends must himself be friendly, but there is a friend who sticks closer than a brother!" Emerging leaders who find the "closer than a brother" friend will ensure themselves of greater leadership stability.

Preferred Mentors / Coaches

Everyone has blind-spots. Places in their personality, their inherent abilities, their communication skills, their self-awareness, and the list goes on. These blind spots are enhanced by the natural tendencies toward comparison and competition. One of the best ways to see and overcome them is to invite a mentor/coach to address them. Most leaders are surrounded by those who readily offer their opinion but a mentor/coach is different. A mentor/coach has no ulterior motives. They win when the leader wins. Yet many leaders are intimidated to invite that type of relationship into their world. They fear being seen as weak or insecure. They perceive a mentor/coach to be an expert who will want to force their experience or solutions upon them. Some resist this type of assistance having had bad experiences with them in their past. Yet the risk of not having a mentor/coach can be much less than the risk of a leader who presumes they have complete perspective (a blind spot).

Coaches/mentors can ask the hard questions that team members resist. One question asked at the right time can make a needed course correction and shift the strategic plan in the right direction. Greater transparency can be achieved in a coaching/mentoring relationship. Remember, the coach/mentor wins when the leader wins.

> Whomever a leader decides to do life with will either open or close doors of opportunity.

Here are some keys to choosing a great coach/mentor partnership.

1. While a mentor/coach does not have to be an expert in your field, they do need to be an experienced and proven leader. A novice cannot ask the right question at the right time.
2. A mentor/coach needs to be relationally oriented but confident enough to ask hard questions. They must have the ability to read the room and discern where honesty needs to be revealed.
3. An experienced mentor/coach will approach the relationship without a set agenda or a predetermined script to work from in order to achieve success. They value their client as the expert in their field and seek only to help them discover the next step in their journey.

4. Mentor/coach relationships have to be embedded with trust. Trust that moves beyond a confidentiality agreement. A client must feel safe, free from judgement, and empowered to uncover personal truth.
5. Sometimes a mentor/coach has to be more than a confidant, a friend, or a guide. They need to be a father/mother figure that can speak from the heart. They can speak into places of the heart that go unnoticed by a peer or a hireling.

It seems natural that **Preferred Mentors / Coaches** would be found within the established leadership community. There is a cry for this type of relationship that reaches deep into the millennial mindset. The difficulty is that many seasoned leaders grew up in what many might refer to as the "John Wayne" culture. Leaders don't cry. Leaders never show weakness. It was a "do as I say" not "as I do" generation. Many of their fathers were involved in WWII and returned scarred and emotionally disconnected. These fathers and grandfathers birthed what has become known as "a fatherless generation." This is now the generation being called upon to provide mentorship and coaching. This is where the leadership gap becomes most evident. Young leaders are hungry to grow, to be fathered, to be coached. Mature leaders afraid they may not have what it takes. Many even unsure of how they arrived without a mentor or coach themselves. SEASONED LEADER CHALLENGE YOURSELF.... THERE IS MORE IN YOU THAN YOU REALIZE!

Piercing Relationships

These are the gold mines! They are few in number but they are crucial to wholeness. Someone said, "A healthy leader builds healthy organizations." Piercing relationships are necessary in order to become healthy and whole. Every leader needs someone who knows them to their core. They need a safe place to unpack the cares of their life. They need a person who is granted access into their soul and spirit. Why? Because anything hidden is a seedbed for failure, for pain, for corruption, for defeat. A secure relationship can bring these issues to light. There are only a few people allowed into this space. They are trusted. They have proven to be loyal. There is no fear present because their love is evident. James, the brother of Jesus Christ, speaks to the benefit of these relationships when he writes, "Confess your faults to one another that you might be healed." James 5:16. Whatever lurks in the dark of a leader's soul is the seedbed for their demise. James says that when you speak out and bring to light what's under the surface, you start a process of healing. What good is it for a leader to climb the ladder of success only to lose their family? Will the prestigious title they earn satisfy them when there are no friends around to celebrate the promotion? Does the wealth accrued merit the scandalous reputation that follows them? Piercing relationships speak the truth in love. They dig into the motives. They challenge integral issues that surface. When a leader responds to the prodding, the poking, the piercing, by taking a truthful examination of their inward person, they position themselves to win their freedom. Bob Hamp, a freedom ministry expert, made the statement that, "Freedom is not the absence of something but the presence of Someone." He was referring to the presence of Jesus Christ. When a friend of Jesus shows up in the person of a piercing relationship, Jesus comes with them. A leader who welcomes them and is willing to confess their inadequacies finds freedom. Free leaders free others in their organization. Piercing relationships are painful on the one hand and healing on the other. They are valuable! They are worth every emerging leader's energy and time to discover. A developing leader who finds this type of relationship will save themselves in both good and bad times.

SEASONED LEADER, CHALLENGE YOURSELF...THERE IS MORE IN YOU THAN YOU REALIZE!

Seasoned leaders may find themselves void of relationships in this arena, simply because they were molded by the previous leadership before them who shied away from intimacy. They were educated under a philosophy promoting disconnect the higher up the leadership ladder one ascended. Executive leadership meant minimizing relationships and guarding against anyone getting too close. What if they were wrong? What if closeness and familiarity could benefit the leader? What if scripture is right when it says, "As iron sharpens iron, so a friend sharpens a friend." Proverbs 27:17 (NLT).

What if a veteran leader took the risk and allowed themselves to invite a young, growing leader into their world? Maybe a new generational transference of leadership could take shape. Maybe the emerging leaders could be developed in the security of a fathering culture. Maybe there would be a resurgence of honor between generations. Maybe a fresh approach to leadership development would reestablish the integrity and character that should define a true leader. Maybe.

Making it Real:

I shared several significant relationships in the Acknowledgements of this book and I hope you read that section. If not, please take time to read it.

I met Paul in 2006. I had recently turned 50 years old and had over thirty years of successful executive level leadership experience. Our meeting was no accident. Although I was fifty years old and had all this success, I was empty inside. I wasn't in a mid-life crisis state. It was deeper than that. The years of fatherlessness, the seasons of being betrayed, the moments I had to be a "hardass" to those under my oversight, the culmination of all the marriage and family stress, and the overall wear and tear of leading were embedded deep in my soul. There never seemed to be a way out of the cycles of criticism, false accusations, pressure, and unreal expectations. Just suck it up and move on. Enduring each situation in hopes that something new would come our way. Constantly looking for breakthrough (whatever that means). That the state I was in when Paul Panquerne showed up. Paul wasn't a professional counselor. He was just an authentic man. He didn't possess any great titles, he wasn't affluent, he didn't have an overwhelming persona, and he wasn't a person who commanded your attention. But he was an authentic man. We became friends and then we became best friends. Paulie, his nickname, became my safe place. He wasn't an accountability partner. He was a man who I could trust completely without reservation. Over the years that have followed our first encounter I have become an authentic man. What do I mean by that, authentic man? There is no place in my life that is hidden. I am no longer posing to impress, to cover up, or to hide. I now walk in freedom because the hidden secrets that I kept in my soul have been brought to light. To some leaders, this will sound like one of those "touchy, feeley" ventures that they vowed never to enter. Good for them. But I am free. I am authentic. I am whole. Paulie was the piercing relationship that I needed for that to happen. I am a better leader. I am a better husband. I am a better father. I am a better friend. Why? Because I have a safe relationship where I do not have to hide. I was a seasoned, successful, tenured leader who was raised by a generation that espoused the theory that leaders lived in isolation. That lie has been broken and I now live a life of relational leadership.

So what is to be learned from my story?

1. Isolation is not healthy for a leader.
2. Authenticity is only discovered in the light.
3. Freedom is worth taking the path of vulnerability and transparency.

Emerging Leaders Action Items:

1. Answer the questions in the section on Purposeful Relationships.
2. Make the hard call about the relationships in your inner circle.

Established Leaders Action Items:

1. Re-read Piercing Relationships and Making It Real.
2. Write a letter to a Piercing Relationship… if you don't have one… imagine what that person would be like and write the letter. Expose yourself in the writing. Truth is your best friend.

Remember:

- ⚲ You cannot lead without key relationships at every level.
- ⚲ To realize maximum potential, a leader must seriously consider who they allow into their inner circle.
- ⚲ Greater transparency can be achieved in a coaching/mentoring relationship.
- ⚲ Every leader needs a secure relationship to unpack the cares of their life.

EIGHT

Self-Leadership Under Pressure

When it comes to leadership, self-leadership seems to be the most difficult to navigate. This is a great truth to be understood early on in a young leader's life. Especially when the pressure seems overwhelming. Those moments in every leader's life when they wonder if they have what it will take. Times when the leader experiences betrayal or is falsely accused. Occasions where expectations are not being met and the team is underperforming. The leader's reactions and responses during those difficult stretches are critical. Leaders must manage their attitudes. They have to navigate their emotions, and they have to temper their conversations. Coach Tom Mullins said, "A leader should live by principles not pressure." Pressure brings out the best and the worst in every leader. Leadership begins within the leader. Emerging leaders who establish a set of personal core values will circumvent many pitfalls. Having pre-set ethics and standards help them temper attitudes, modify reactions, and overcome personal faults. It is vital to understand that only the leader can govern their own soul and lead themselves through leadership pressure and pain.

Before any personal leadership crisis, the wise leader works to predetermine their response. It all starts with the moral standards they establish, the values that set the borders of their spiritual priorities, their emotional well-being, and their relational responses. Under pressure the heart of the leader is coaxed to believe a lie. Jeremiah 17:9 says, "The human heart is the most deceitful of all things, and desperately wicked. Who really knows how bad it is?" This is never truer than in seasons of personal stress, when the heart and mind want to whisper things like; "just this once" or "no one will know" or "I'm not hurting anyone." A wise leader has already answered those questions... No! No, because they decided a course of action prior to any personal leadership temptation. No, because they have done the work to strengthen their principles. No, because they build fortresses around those principles in their hearts and minds. It is so essential that values govern the leader's personal life. Think about the moral failures of prominent leaders in both the marketplace and the church. It only takes one moment of weakness, one minute of self-doubt, one second of believing a lie, and all the progress of the past comes tumbling down. The leader's ethical compass must continually be fortified and calibrated to address new seasons of influence, promotion, and opportunity. Each level brings new temptations that seek for a prime opening to slay the leader. No level of leadership is immune from the depravity of the human heart. However, novice leaders who fail to establish moral borders early on make themselves extremely vulnerable.

The art of leading oneself is genuinely tested in the context of team dynamics. Leaders are challenged when deadlines are imminent and there seems to be a lack of urgency among group members. Leadership becomes difficult when silos are built between departments leading to competition and politics.

Teams can also create personal difficulties for leaders if gossip and undermining creep into the organization. Leaders must exercise self-restraint when these and other issues surface within group relations. Factions within an organization can crush a leader who failed to form the disciplines necessary to lead with confidence. Self-leadership emboldens and empowers the leader to lead their team, their department, their company, or their church through these difficult moments and times. The foundations of the leader will become evident because they will lead from their core principles. People respond to a leader who is confident and retains convictions. Teams unravel under leaders who show favoritism, lack ethics, promote self, blame others, or refuse to own their own poor decisions.

> Before any personal
> leadership crisis,
> the wise leader
> works to
> predetermine their
> response.

So how can leaders emerge unscathed? What will keep them, so they experience a long and effective leadership tenure. The Psalmist gives a great starting place, Psalms 119:11 "I have hidden Your word in my heart, that I might not sin against You." The precedence of God's Word in a leader's life will help establish the foundation of ethics necessary to lead effectively. This is more than reading the Bible. This is building leadership values within the context of a biblical worldview. This is belief. This is a firm conviction. This is being fully persuaded that His

Word is truth and is relevant to leadership. So, when the wind of adversity blows, the biblical response is encoded in the DNA of the leader. Like Joseph, the leader runs from the enticer and keeps their integrity intact. Unlike Peter, the leader stands when they face accusers and does not offer excuses. Like Esther, they are willing to risk everything to fulfill their purpose. Unlike the children of Israel, they are not fearful of giants and walled cities but rather they take on the future with confidence. These leaders lead in difficult times. These leaders know what to do and how to inspire others to journey with them. These leaders stand in the face of their enemies and overcome because these leaders live by principles not pressure.

Leadership is often threatened by one person. The one leading. The one with the sign on their desk: "The buck stops here!" Many times, it is because of their pride, their demands for entitlement, their ability to control, or simply their lack of integrity. A closer look may reveal that those are only the fruit of what is really the root. Underneath the surface there can be an orphaned mentality. A perspective that craves approval and has a deep-rooted need for the affirmation of others. A cry for respect expressed through an excessive competitive nature. They are obsessed with comparison and measure their success against others for validation. A leader of this nature has imprisoned themselves to their personal perceived value. They lean heavily into how they feel others see them.

Saul is a great example of a leader who damaged his own leadership. Even when he was to be anointed to be king he was hiding among the baggage. He never really accepted God's call on him to lead. He succumbed to the will of the people and disobeyed God's instructions. Later Saul became threatened by the praises given to David. He threw spears at David and chased David to kill him. Then he put the nail in the coffin by consulting the witch of Endor. All of this may have been avoided had he been able to see himself in a different light. His insecurity destroyed him, and he lost the kingdom as a result.

Leaders must navigate the way ahead. They must identify the destination and define the reason for going there. If the team never knows where they are going, then how will they know when they arrive? And if the leader is unable to articulate the objective, he will soon be subjugated to the leading of others. People are uncomfortable with ambiguity. Leaders must have a well-defined purpose and confidently communicate it so that others will follow. An effective leader can paint the picture of the future because they see it clearly. Robert Morris, Lead Pastor of Gateway Church, offers this advice to leaders looking for direction, "God wants us to lead by hearing His voice."

A spiritual leader seeks God first. While they may have access to data, beta testing, and wise counsel, they know true discernment of the future is best had by spending time with God. Their practice is to look to heaven daily because they know they cannot delegate prayer. They have faith that God still speaks today. Spiritual leaders know they can't afford to live in the past. They realize a new day brings the need for a new strategy and maybe a course correction. So, their first objective is to hear His voice.

Spiritual leaders also approach the future by faith. They believe God will provide everything needed to succeed. There is a confidence to move forward because they know God has set the course. They know that He is Jehovah Jireh, the Lord Who goes ahead to provide. David modeled this type of faith when he went out to meet Goliath. David recalled the past; I have killed a lion and a bear. He knew what God had done but at this moment he needed to know what God would do. Where the power of memory allowed him to replay past victories, the power of faith allowed him to pre-play what God was about to do. "I come to you in the name of the God of Israel... and today I am going to take your head off and feed it to the ravens." Spiritual leaders have faith in what God said and lead from that vantage point.

> The precedence of God's Word in a leader's life will help establish the foundation of ethics necessary to lead effectively.

Spiritual leaders are quick to obey. They have disciplined their lives to respond to God's instructions with an immediate "yes." They may not comprehend everything but they know understanding can wait however, obedience cannot. Enterprises done God's way and in God's timing will succeed. The key is the obedience of the leader. A disciplined listener, a person of unquestionable faith, and a leader who willingly submits to the Spirit will surely do great things.

All leaders are tested when they must navigate through periods of uncertainty. These are seasons where a leap into the unknown is being required but the outcome is unsure. Some would call this, "the place in between" and it looks like this;

after you jump but before you land. The place in between is scary. Decisions made here will either catapult the leader's influence or empower thoughts of failure. It's in this gap that great leaders perform.

The battlefield in uncertain times is crucial ground. The leader will either lean into fear or stay confident in faith. Fear and faith are both fighting for footing. Motivation is at risk. Emotions are stretched. Self-leadership is questioned. As well, severe external challenges can emerge during these "*middle moments.*" And leaders must sustain their momentum, maintain their poise, and lead forward with strength. They must be able to look insecurity in the face and say, "I've got this!"

Paul writes Timothy from prison to give him some encouragement. His words to Timothy have some advice relevant to the middle moments. First, leaders must never forget they are gifted to lead. When times are uncertain there will be many voices. And while leaders should take counsel to heart, in the end, they have to step up and lead. Paul reminds Timothy not to forget the spiritual gift imparted to him by others. Leaders are anointed to lead. Secondly, Timothy is admonished to recognize that "God has not given him a spirit of fear and timidity, but of power, love, and self-discipline." 2 Timothy 1:7. Right or wrong, the leader must step up and lead boldly through the fog without regard to what others think or say. An insecure leader will be eaten alive by the voice of the multitude or the nay-sayers. At that moment he will no longer be the leader but the follower. Lastly, Paul exhorts young Timothy to lead from the position of sound doctrine and the power of the Holy Spirit. Leaders lead through the place called "in between" when they know how to get wisdom from God's word and yield to the power of the Holy Spirit. God's Word establishes the principles of life to make wise decisions. The power of the Holy Spirit guides the leader to truth and provides the wherewithal to weather the emotional upheaval. All leaders have to make a jump into the unknown at some point. What they do before they land will set the organization up for success or failure. The "in between" will identify those courageous enough to lead with confidence.

> Leaders must have a
> well-defined purpose
> and confidently
> communicate it so
> that others will
> follow.

Making it Real:

In 2016 I was a part of a major downsizing along with 300 other employees. Having been a part of the senior management team, I understood all the reasons for the cuts. I fully supported the actions needed at that time to take the organization forward. Now I found myself a part of those decisions. It was difficult to hear the news. **Let me throw this thought in right here, "The way you leave a season, is the way you will enter the next season.** I was 61 at the time and I must admit I was very uncertain and concerned about what my future held. The battle with fear and the struggle with my self-worth were daily challenges for a season. I would love to say I was a man of steel and fully confident. But I wasn't. However, I can say that I immediately began to lean on the core values and principles to fight through the unknown. Philippians 4:6-7 says, "Don't worry about anything; instead pray about everything. Tell God what you need, and thank Him for all He has done. Then you will experience God's peace, which exceeds anything we can understand. His peace will guard your hearts and minds as you live in Christ Jesus." Peace became my first anchor. Proverbs 3:5-6 says, "Trust in the Lord with all your heart; do not depend on our own understanding. Seek His will in all you do, and He will show you which path to take." Trust in God was my second source of strength. I recalled the times He had sustained us and never let us go without. I remembered a time when he asked us to leave a place where we were very comfortable and successful. We moved 1,100 miles away to start over completely without a job offer or promise of one. He never failed us and He would not fail us in this transition. Lastly, I worshipped Him. Psalms 59:17, "O my Strength, to You I sing praises, for You, O God, are my refuge, The God who shows me unfailing love." This probably sounds crazy to sum. But I did not renew my resume. I didn't recruit a staffing agency. I never jumped on LinkedIn and searched for opportunities. I simply walked in His peace, trusted His will for my life, and worshipped Him for His faithfulness to us. Today I find myself on the other side of that transition and I am living the most fulfilling life. I started a company called Bogard Group, I assist in leading a network of international non-profits, and I am writing books. What looked like one of the worst days of my life was really the catalyst for the greatest days of my life.

So what is to be learned from my story?

1. On the other side of pressure and difficulty there are opportunities that will only be unlocked or missed by the choices you make in the midst of the struggle.
2. You will live out what you believe to be true.

Emerging Leaders Action Items:

1. What areas of your life do you need to strengthen in order to lead under pressure?
2. Identify the character strengths that you acquired from your family, your education, your mentor, or your experience.
3. Make a list of people you admire for their self-leadership.
4. Beside each person's name define the leadership quality.
5. Now describe how you can apply it in your life.

Established Leaders Action Items:

1. What "middle moments" have you experienced? How did you manage the transition?
2. Write a training session that addresses self-leadership.
3. Present it in a staff meeting.

Remember:

- Before any personal leadership crisis, the wise leader works to predetermine their response.
- The art of leading oneself is genuinely tested in the context of team dynamics.
- Leadership is often threatened by one person. The one leading.
- Leaders must navigate the way ahead. They must identify the destination and define the reason for going there.
- Leaders must sustain their momentum, maintain their poise, and lead forward with strength.

SELF LEADERSHIP UNDER PRESSURE

NINE

Understanding Your Worldview

Every leader leads from a certain worldview. Young leaders should choose early on what worldview will drive their philosophy of leadership. There are two worldviews to choose from and each of those contain two streams of thought. These two perspectives of life are spiritual and humanistic. Viewing the world through a spiritual lens establishes a higher power (God) as the source of truth and the center of all life. Contrasting is the theory that mankind is central to all life and science as the source to truth. Spiritual leaders choose to lead from either a biblical worldview or from a religious mindset. On the other hand, someone leading from a humanistic worldview seeks self-realization through either power or asceticism. The focus here will be on a biblical worldview.

A biblical worldview acknowledges God as the means to truth and purpose. It espouses that wisdom. That the ability to apply knowledge and experience to one's everyday life comes from a revelation of God's nature and character. Revelation is acquired through a personal relationship with the God of the Bible. The Bible is God's word to man and contains the blueprint for a life of purpose and meaning. Therefore,

Christian leadership is character leadership influenced by biblical principles. The personal revelation of those principles is given to them by the Holy Spirit of God. A biblical worldview leader therefore prioritizes their daily life, their family values, and their occupational pursuits to fall in line with fundamental biblical truths.

Every leader leads
from a certain
worldview.

The central truths that emerge regarding leadership with a biblical worldview would be:

→ **_Servant leadership_**, which is based upon Jesus statement, "But among you it will be different. Whoever wants to be a leader among you must be your servant, and whoever wants to be first among you must be the slave of everyone else. For even the Son of Man came not to be served but to serve others and to give His life as a ransom for many." Mark 10:43-45. A servant leader will never be a top down leader who uses their authority and title to push their personal agenda. Servant leadership understands that authority is gained by empowering others to reach their full potential. Leaders who make it more about the mission and their team than the role they play, demonstrate the nature of biblical leadership centered in the attitude of serving. Their world view looks through the lens of the Bible and motivates them to help others in their world become better. They are more inclined to take up the towel of a servant than the robe of a king. These leaders understand that pushing others forward inevitably results in their personal mission being realized.

→ ***Kingdom minded leadership*** which acknowledges God is King over all and owns it all. It is leadership that seeks after God's agenda and refuses to allow the "ROI" and the bottom line on the balance sheet to be their definition of success. Paul put kingdom minded leadership into perspective when he wrote this to the church at Rome; "God's Kingdom isn't a matter of what you put in your stomach, for goodness's sake. It's what God does with your life as He sets it right, puts it together, and completes it with joy. Your task is to single-mindedly serve Christ. Do that and you'll kill two birds with one stone: pleasing the God above you and proving your worth to the people around you." Romans 14:17,18 (Message Bible) A kingdom leader seeks to do business in a righteous manner and with impeccable integrity. They seek to be peacemakers and lead teams relationally, so that the outcome is beneficial to all. These leaders are motivated to see God's will be done on earth in a way that others are benefited by the provisions of God's Kingdom. They are not intimidated by the success of others. They seek collaboration for the welfare of the community. Kingdom minded leaders compete with adversaries but celebrate the success of colleagues. The Kingdom of God is primary in decision making, strategic planning, and future development. A kingdom leader seeks God first. They are driven to discover His plan and committed to its implementation. His Kingdom is primary. He is Lord. He is the Creator. He is the Beginning and He is the End. The heart cry of a kingdom leader is, "May His Kingdom come, may His Will be done, on earth as it is in Heaven!"

→ ***Spirit-led Leadership*** focuses on the integration of both the Spirit and the attributes given to leaders by their Creator. Spirit-led leaders rely on God's spirit and Word to give them guidance. Some scriptures that support that train of thought would be:

◆ Proverbs 3:5,6 (Message Bible) "Trust God from the bottom of your heart; don't try to figure out everything on your own. Listen for God's voice in everything you do, everywhere you go; He is the one who will keep you on track."

◆ Psalm 37:23 (NLT) "The Lord directs the steps of the godly. He delights in every detail of their lives."

However, there is also an understanding that each leader is endowed with certain skills and aptitudes which enable them to lead naturally. The proficiency to communicate, the ability to devise strategic initiatives, the talent to build teams, the competence to create delivery systems, or the genius to solve difficult problems are all natural capabilities that allow leaders to produce whenever they are asked to lead. Paul speaks to this in 1 Corinthians 12:28 (NLT) Here are some of the parts God has appointed for the church: "First are apostles, second are prophets, third are teachers, then those who do miracles, those who have the gift of healing, those who can help others, those who have the gift of leadership, those who speak in unknown languages." God gave gifts to each person for their unique purpose in life. It would be foolish for a leader not to lean into their natural strengths. However, it would be foolish for a leader with a biblical worldview to rely solely on those talents. They understand at some junctures they need the assistance of the Holy Spirit. These men and women understand that part of the Holy Spirit's job description is to lead them into truth. The Holy Spirit was given to the church as a guide, a counselor, and a personal instructor. His presence is always with spirit-led leaders. When they seek Him, He answers and brings clarity of purpose and direction. The Holy Spirit knows God's perfect will in any situation and can help leaders navigate the nuances of life to discover it. A leaders' best day of decision-making pales in comparison to one moment of the Spirit's directives. This is seen in the life of Joseph. The king's confidants and wise men were stunned and in total confusion by the king's dream. When Joseph was summoned from the prison, he had the interpretation from God's spirit. Joseph was exalted to rule as second only to the king. Scripture is full of other examples where the Holy Spirit directed the champions and heroes of the Bible to accomplish their missions. Spirit-led leaders believe and adhere to the truth that the same Holy Spirit speaks today. They understand that human talent alone can fall short. They trust the Holy Spirit's leading in those moments of confusion.

While one could elaborate on a number of other biblical leadership concepts, these seem to surface as the most essential.

> A biblical worldview acknowledges God as the means to truth and purpose.

A biblical worldview begins with a personal relationship with the God of the Bible. This is where a line is drawn between a religious biblical worldview and a relational worldview. Religion is a pursuit to appease the demands of a transcendent God who stays detached from human affairs. God is viewed as demanding a set of rules be adhered to or else there are consequences to pay. Religion focuses on the works that men and women do to acquire a right standing with God and thus earn their way into whatever eternal future lies ahead. Religion tends to be judgmental and burdensome. It requires a sense of perfectionism. Redemption seems unachievable because there is always something that could be done better or some other demand that must be met.

Flip the coin. A biblical worldview based upon a relationship with God looks completely different. This model is God initiated. God saw that mankind had put themselves in a state where they were separated from Him. Their transgressions were unable to be reconciled by working their way to righteousness. Therefore, God made the decision to redeem mankind from their condition. He chose to come in the form of a human, to suffer as a human, and to do the work of salvation as a human. He did this through His only Son Jesus Christ.

> The Holy Spirit
> knows God's perfect
> will in any situation
> and can help leaders
> navigate the nuances
> of life to discover it.

The most well-known verse in the Bible records this gracious act of God's kindness. John 3:16, "For this is how God loved the world. He gave His one and only Son, so that everyone who believes in Him will not perish but have eternal life." Most readers stop there but the next verse really speaks to the heart and attitude of this amazing gift. John 3:17, "God did not send His Son into the world to condemn it, but in order that the world might be saved through Him." Stop. Think about what was just communicated. God wasn't looking for a way to make the world pay for their sin. He did not relish the opportunity to hold something against them. Rather, He wanted to restore, to heal, to provide a way for mankind to be connected to Him. That way was Jesus, His only Son. Romans 5:8 clearly communicates this heartfelt attitude, "But God put His love on the line for us by offering His Son in sacrificial death while we were of no use whatever to Him." (Message Bible).

Now the question surfaces, how does a person enter into this relationship. It's really simple. Romans 10:9,10 declares, "If you confess with your mouth the Lord Jesus and believe in your heart that God raised Him from the dead, you will be saved. For with the heart one believes unto righteousness, and with the mouth confession is made unto salvation."

Step one: Decide to believe in your heart and soul that what Jesus did to pay for your salvation has validity.

Step two: Choose to receive the gift of Jesus' sacrifice as payment for all the things that have separated you from God.

Step Three: Let God and man know you have made that decision. Let God know by a simple prayer: "God I believe You gave Jesus as a sacrifice for all my sins. I believe You want to change my life for the better. I believe You have a purpose for me and I want to live that purpose. So today I open my heart and soul to Jesus to make Jesus the Lord and Master of my life. From this day forward, I will live to please You and fulfill your plan for me. AMEN." Then you can let people know by telling them you have made this decision. A great place to start that conversation is with other people who have made that same decision. Look for a life-giving church. You will know its life-giving when you get there because the people will not be religious. They won't be looking to perfect you. They will be excited to walk with you and help you learn to live out your faith. They will help you when you don't get it right all the time. They will help you understand that sometimes it's ok if you are not ok. Just be on the journey to become ok!

A biblical worldview
begins with a
personal
relationship with the
God of the Bible.

If you made that decision today, please let us know. If not, please let us know how we can pray for you. Know you are loved. Know you are special. Know you are welcome to continue the search for truth. We won't throw stones at you. If you are on the path of relationship with Him, please make His renown known to those you do life with at work, in your neighborhood, and wherever you meet others. You can reach us at welcomehome@bogardgroup.com.

Making it Real:

I have a great friend who has been like a son to me in many ways but also a mentor. He is an entrepreneur and has started a few successful businesses. We have had many conversations about **"Christian Leaders or Business Owners."** One particular business he had was to provide resources to have a solid online presence. Many of his customers proclaimed their business or product to be **"Christian."** However, their business practices and financial integrity were lacking. I have heard that related to me from several other prominent businesses. It pains me to write this. There is no defense for these types of practices. The bible itself exhorts us to honor our word even if it is to our own detriment. I know these are not the actions of all Christian businesses or leaders but it is regrettable that even one would mis-represent the values and principles of true Christianity. If you have been disappointed by your dealings with these poor representatives of Christ, I want to say I am sorry. I am sorry they did not honor their word. I am sorry that they did not pay their bills. I am sorry that they broke their contract. I am sorry that you had to write off their debt. I am sorry that you walked away from that experience with a bad taste in your mouth for Christians. My hope is that this book has inspired you to believe that their actions did not represent all. That you can see in this writing the challenges that will shape strong emerging leaders. My desire is that we can bridge the gap between generations of leaders and restore the integrity of doing business and leading with integrity.

So what is to be learned from my story?

1. If you talk the talk then walk the walk.
2. Leave Christ's name out if His morals are not in play.
3. Build your business and lead from your real worldview.

Emerging Leaders Action Items:

1. Define your worldview.
2. How does your worldview shape your leadership?

Established Leaders Action Items:

1. Define your worldview.
2. How does your worldview shape your leadership?

Remember:

- Young leaders should choose early on what worldview will drive their philosophy of leadership.
- Servant leadership understands that authority is gained by empowering others to reach their full potential.
- A kingdom leader seeks to do business in a righteous manner and with impeccable integrity.
- Spirit-led leaders understand that human talent alone can fall short.

360° Masterplan

The 360° Masterplan is a proven strategy to give you the direction, health and increase you desire. We provide various levels of coaching that include onsite and online assessments to take your organization to the win it deserves.

EXECUTIVE LEVEL (1YR COACHING PLAN)

- 360° Church Health Survey
- 3 Days On-site with Your Leadership
- Full Day of On-site Leadership Evaluation
- 2 Days of Follow-up Either On-site or Over Video
- 10 Monthly Video Coaching Calls

PREMIUM LEVEL (3 MONTH COACHING PLAN)

- 3 Days On-site with Your Leadership
- Full Day of Strategic Plan Evaluation
- 2 Hour Video Conference Coaching with Team Leads
- 3 Monthly Video Coaching Calls

ADDITIONAL CONSULTING OPTIONS

- Personal 1-on-1 Coaching
- In-person or Video Call Coaching
- By Yourself or with Your Spouse

SCHEDULE YOUR FREE CONSULTATION TODAY

BOGARDGROUP.COM

ABOUT THE AUTHOR

Bobby Bogard has over 45 years of ministry that spans a broad range of specialized areas within church and non-profit organizations. His experience includes 25 years of senior level leadership within mega-church and multi-site environments. Bobby has been a "pastor to pastors" throughout his ministry. His calling is to be a "father to the fatherless". He is passionate about approaching leadership from a generational perspective.

Bobby and his wife, Rose (better known as The Beautiful Rose of Texas), founded The Bogard Group because they believe "Every Leader Matters". The Bogards never want to see a leader or pastor lead alone. They desire to maximize their comprehensive experience to see every leader and organization achieve the passionate mission that compelled them to exist. They believe healthy growing leaders will lead healthy growing churches and organizations which are the hope of the world!

UNDERSTANDING YOUR WORLDVIEW